Elijah
THE PROPHET

Elijah
THE PROPHET

BY THE

REV. WILLAM M. TAYLOR D.D.

AMBASSADOR
BELFAST ◆ **GREENVILLE**
NORTHERN IRELAND **SOUTH CAROLINA**

First Published 1889
This edition 1997

ISBN   1 898787 25 5

AMBASSADOR PRODUCTIONS LTD,
Providence House
16 Hillview Avenue,
Belfast, BT5 6JR
Northern Ireland

Emerald House,
1 Chick Springs Road, Suite 206
Greenville,
South Carolina 29609
United States of America

PREFACE

To read a part of the Old Testament in the light of the New, and to discover in it, when thus treated, not only a portion of the history of the past, but also the explanation of much that is in the present, and the prophecy of more that is in the future, is the aim of this book.

The story of Elijah is one of thrilling interest. There is a shadow of mystery, and yet a mien of majesty, about the hero which so affects every reader, that he is almost apt to forget that the Tishbite was, after all, 'a man subject to like passions as we are.' I have endeavoured, by setting the prophet amidst the surroundings of his age, and comparing him with the reformers of other days, to bring him so near to us, that we may hear the throb of his great heart and catch the inspiration of his life. I have not attempted to conceal his failings, but have sought everywhere to draw from his conduct the lessons most appropriate to our modern circumstances.

The kind reception given to 'David, King of Israel,' has encouraged me to send forth this new work; and if it shall awaken any to earnest study of the Word of God, or give direction and support to any perplexed or fainting spirit, I will be devoutly thankful.

Wm. M. Taylor
Broadway Tabernacle
December 3rd, 1875

CONTENTS

ELIJAH THE PROPHET.

—o—

I.

THE STARTLING MESSAGE.

1 KINGS xvii. 1.

ISRAEL was at this time in a most deplorable
condition. Its rulers had caused the nation to
err; and as one king after another disappears from
the scene, his character and history are summed up
by the sacred chronicler in the words, "He did evil
in the sight of Jehovah after the manner of Jeroboam
the son of Nebat, who made Israel to sin." This is
the sad refrain continually recurring in the national
annals, and each time it is repeated it reveals a
blacker depth of wickedness than before. Of Omri
it had been said that "he did worse than all that
were before him;" but it was reserved for Ahab to
inaugurate a new species of iniquity, more revolting than any which the ten tribes had committed
since the date of their rebellion against the son of
Solomon.

This monarch was by no means the weakling he is

commönly supposed to have been. Now and again,
indeed, his whole nature seems to have been, for the
time, paralysed under the operation of what Maurice
has described as "a troublesome conscience, checking
an evil will;"[1] but in general he manifested those
qualities which have secured for other kings the title
"great." He was brave and successful on the field
of battle. Once and again he vanquished the army
of the proud Ben-hadad;[2] and at last he met his
death while fighting valiantly, though in disguise, at
Ramoth-gilead.[3] This personal prowess was combined in him with a love of art and a desire to
promote the commercial prosperity of his people.
He made streets for himself in the great trading city
of Damascus.[4] He reared for himself a palace of
ivory, and was, besides, the founder of several cities.[5]
But all this outward magnificence was dimmed by a
darker shadow of iniquity than that which fell on the
glory of any of his predecessors. Thus it is written
concerning him : "It came to pass, as if it had been
a light thing for him to walk in the sins of Jeroboam
the son of Nebat, that he took to wife Jezebel the
daughter of Ethbaal king of the Zidonians, and went
and served Baal, and worshipped him. And he reared
up an altar for Baal in the house of Baal, which he had
built in Samaria. And Ahab made a grove ; and Ahab
did more to provoke the Lord God of Israel to anger
than all the kings of Israel that were before him."[6]

---

[1] "The Prophets and Kings of the Old Testament," by F. D.
Maurice, p. 129.   [2] 1 Kings xx. 21-29.
      [3] Ibid., xxii. 34.   [4] Ibid., xx. 34.
      [5] Ibid.; xxii. 39 ; Amos iii. 15. [6] 1 Kings xvi. 31-33.

There is thus a clear distinction drawn between the sin of Jeroboam and that of Ahab. It is intimated that, as the son of Nebat took a new departure from the worship at Jerusalem, when he set up the gólden calves at Dan and at Bethel, so the son of Omri took a new departure from the practice of Jeroboam, when he built a temple and set up an altar to Baal. The act of Jeroboam was, in the main, political. He foresaw that if the tribes who had chosen him to be their king continued to go to Jerusalem to attend the three great annual religious festivals, the spiritual union would speedily overcome the political division. So he established separate centres of worship at Bethel and Dan ; and knowing the craving of the heart for some visible emblem of the Divine glory, he set up the Egyptian symbol of the calf. He could not have the real shechinah, but he did set up an outward representation ; and his particular selection of the calf may be traced to the influence upon him of Egyptian ideas consequent upon his long residence as an exile in that land. But he had no desire to give up the covenant claim of the people on Jehovah. Indeed, he would not have admitted that he had ceased to serve Jehovah. His view of the case was that he was serving Jehovah under the symbol of the golden calf; and therefore the sin which he committed was not a violation of the first commandment, but of the second. He had not a thought of worshipping any other god than Jehovah ; but he guiltily made to himself and to his people an outward symbol to represent Jehovah. That was bad enough ; but the guilt of Ahab was greatly more heinous, for he abjured Jehovah altogether, denying His exclusive claim to deity, and repudiating anything like a covenant relationship between Him and Israel.

He thus dethroned Jehovah, and on the vacant seat he placed Baal and Ashtaroth, the two divinities of the Zidonians. These were the deities of the old Canaanites, for their homage to which these ancient tribes were driven out to make way for the descendants of Abraham. Hence, the adoption of their worship by the ten tribes was a total apostasy from Jehovah, and a return to the ancient idolatry of the land. It was not merely a violation of the second commandment, in that there was an image of Baal in stone, and of Ashtaroth in wood ; but it was also a breaking of the first commandment, in that it involved the repudiation of Jehovah, and the adoption of another god in His room. And so Ahab, who introduced this new sort of idolatry, did worse than all that had gone before him.

Now, these two deities, Baal, the male, and Ashtaroth, the female, represented the fertilising and productive principle in nature, and their worship was that of power. To the more cultivated and refined, it was simply a species of Pantheism ; to the multitude, it was what one has called " the worship of deified abundance, under a splendid and sensuous ceremonial ; "[1] or, as Maurice has put it, " The worship of Baal was the worship of power as distinguished from righteousness." [2] Hence, the apostasy of Ahab in giving up the personal Jehovah, the covenant God of Israel, and the Creator and Preserver of all things,

---

[1] " Elijah."   Four University Sermons, by Walter W. Shirley, M.A., Oxford, p. 20.

[2] " The Prophets and Kings of the Old Testament," p. 128.

and preferring Baal, was analogous to, if not, indeed, precisely identical with, the modern heresy of those who discard a personal God, and refuse to believe in Him who is a loving Father, while they deify Nature under the name of Law. Thus this old history has a special appropriateness to the present time, and we may profitably ponder for a little the record of the manner in which the efforts of Ahab were counteracted and neutralised.

The introduction of Baal-worship into Israel was part of a deliberate plan on the part of Ahab. He wished to strengthen himself to the fullest extent against his Syrian enemies, while, at the same time, he developed the material resources of his country by an alliance with the Zidonians, who held the seaboard. If he could only succeed in welding Israel and Zidon together, he felt that he could defy the dynasty of Damascus, and look forward to a time of great prosperity from a participation in the unrivalled commerce of the Phœnicians. But there is no unifying influence so strong as that of religion. Hence he determined to carry the nation over bodily into the Zidonian worship ; and, as the first step in that direction, he allied himself to the royal house of Zidon, by marrying Jezebel, the daughter of Ethbaal, king of the Zidonians.

Thus, if I have read the record aright, his worship of Baal was not the result of his marriage with Jezebel, but his marriage with her was the consequence of his determination to establish Baal-worship throughout his dominions. For political reasons, Jeroboam set up his calves ; and now again, for political reasons, Ahab determines to convert the nation into worshippers of Baal. In this effort he found Jezebel a most efficient and unscrupulous assistant. She was the daughter of one who, being himself a priest of Baal, had, as Josephus[1] tells us, murdered his own brother in order to gain the crown ; so that he was both priest of Baal and king of Zidon. She inherited both the religious fervour of the priest and the unscrupulous cruelty of the man. She united in herself the strongest intellectual powers, the fiercest passions, and the fieriest will, while her moral sense was hardened almost into insensibility. With her, "I dare not" never waited upon " I would ; " and, no matter what stood in the way of the attainment of her designs, she would trample down every obstacle, and press forward, even through " a mire of blood," to the object of her ambition. She may be regarded as the Lady Macbeth of history ; only, as it seems to me, there was less of " the milk of human kindness " in her breast than the great dramatist has put into that of his striking creation ; and Jezebel would not have come back, shivering, with the dry dagger in her hand, saying, " Had he not resembled my father as he slept, I'd done it." Without the least misgiving she would have plunged it into the sleeper to the hilt ! With such an ally, the Baal mission made great progress. The people, indeed, were largely ready for such idolatry. Their hearts had long been set on outward magnificence and power ; and so, in accepting Baal for their god, they only gave their outward homage where they had long been giving their inward adora-

---

[1] "Antiquities," viii. 13, 1 ; contra Appion, i. 18. In the atter citation we identify Ethbaal with Ithobalos.

tion ; and the mass of the community made no complaint when they saw well-nigh a thousand priests supported from the royal funds.[1] A nation which could
see unmoved the rebuilding of Jericho in defiance of
the curse pronounced by Joshua upon him who should
again set up its gates,[2] had evidently swung very far
from its allegiance to Jehovah, and would not hesitate
to follow the example of the court ; for, as all colours
are alike in the dark, so any religion is indifferent to
him who cares nothing for religion at all. There
were, indeed, some faithful among the faithless ; for
even after a bloody persecution, seven thousand remained who had not bowed the knee to Baal, and
among these were a hundred prophets who had
hidden themselves in a cave.[3] But the majority—
belonging to that class so well described by M.
Prochet[4] as "having the religion of 'I don't care,'"
and as having this characteristic, that, while they
would not erect the gibbet or the scaffold for others,
they would by no means face either for themselves—
followed the court, and saw without remark the
emissaries of Jezebel go through the land, overturning
the many altars which had been erected to the one
true God, and hunting down the stern old covenanters
of their day, who would not give homage to the
Zidonian deity.

So, on the whole, the transition had been made
with ease and success ; and Ahab and Jezebel might
be sitting in their Jezreel palace of ivory, congratulat-
ing themselves on the skill which they had shown,

---

[1] I Kings xviii. 19.   [2] Ibid., xvi. 34.   [3] Ibid., xviii. 4 ; xix. 18.
[4] In his address at the Evangelical Alliance, New York ;
October 1873.

when, sudden and terrible as a clap of thunder from
a cloudless sky, there swept in before them a weird-
looking man, with long, flowing hair, a mantle of
sheep-skin round his shoulders, and a rugged staff in
his hand ; and before they could ask him who he was,
or why he had come thither, he had flung the gage
of defiance at their feet, and said, "As Jehovah the
God of Israel liveth, before whom I stand, there shall
not be dew nor rain these years but according to my
word." Then, this message given, he vanished like
an apparition. "It was," as Wilberforce has said,
"like the flash of the lightning, sharp as a blazing
sword in its sudden vividness, but not tarrying for a
moment, revealing everything, and gone as it reveals
it."[1] Who was this strange, uncourtly, and defiant
visitor? All we know of him up till this time is expressed in the words, "Elijah the Tishbite, who was
of the inhabitants of Gilead." No flourish of trumpets ushered him into the presence of royalty ; and
in like manner, no herald precedes him on the sacred
page to proclaim his parentage, or tell the story of his
early life. He is the "Melchizedek" among the
prophets, "without father, without mother, having
neither beginning of days nor end of life, abiding a
prophet continually." And all this is in keeping with
his rugged character, his abrupt and startling appearances, and the stern work he had to do. We know
something of the early history of Moses at the court
of Pharaoh, and we read with interest the narrative of
little Samuel's sojourn at the tabernacle in Shiloh ; we

---

[1] "Heroes of Hebrew History," by Samuel Wilberforce,
D.D., p. 328.

have a glimpse of Elisha at the plough, and of Amos following his herd, ere yet they were called to carry the message of the Lord to the people of the land. But the boyhood and youth of Elijah are unknown. He comes here as suddenly into view as if he had just descended from the clouds, and clothed himself with their thunder as he came ; or we might almost fancy that he had at that moment alighted from the chariot of fire, which, tarrying for him in the heavens, was to bear him ultimately from the earth.

In the absence of all other details, we are glad to make the most we can of his name and designation. Elijah means " My god is Jehovah ; " and this, whether given him by his parents or assumed by himself, was in striking accord with the mission on which he was sent. The very mention of it was a solemn protest against the Baal-homage of Ahab and his court ; and every repetition of it would be to the prophet himself a new reminder of the truth which he had to proclaim, and of the strength by which he would be upheld.

He is called also "The Tishbite." This is supposed by some, rather artificially, as I think, to mean "reformer ; " by others, it is thought to be derived from the place of his residence or of his birth. But we do not know certainly that there was such a place as Thisbe ; and if there even was, it is now impossible to identify it, so that here again we are in the dark. The probability is, that his youthful days were spent in the obscurity of some mountain village, and in the humble lot of poverty. But this is no unusual in the history of God's most distinguished servants. We have spoken already of Amos and

Elisha; can we forget in the same connection a
higher than either, even the Lord Jesus himself,
who was for a time a Galilean · carpenter? The
strongest trees are found, not in sheltered nooks,
but in the most exposed places, where sweeps the
full fury of the storm ; the hardiest flowers grow, not
in the hot-house, but on the mountain-side, in close
proximity to the glacier and the snow ; and God's
grandest heroes are taken, for the most part, not
from the lap of luxury or the home of affluence, but
from the dwelling of penury and the abode of
obscurity.   Their very struggles have developed
strength ; and the difficulties which they have been
forced to encounter have quickened inventiveness and
inspired resolution.

But Elijah was "of the inhabitants of Gilead."
And this, too, may have had some influence in producing that rugged strength which we discern in his
character ; for, surely, the scenery on which one
daily looks has much to do with the formation of
the man.   There is a difference between the hardy
Swiss and the effeminate Italian ; and in the grizzly
visage and patient endurance of the Scottish High-
lander we can see something of the heath-clad
granite of his native hills.   Now, Gilead, on the
eastern side of the Jordan, was a land much like theirs.
"It was," says Mr. Grove, "a country of chase and
pasture, of tent-villages and mountain-castles, in-
habited by a people, not settled and civilised, like
those who formed the communities of Ephraim and
Judah, but of wandering, irregular habits, exposed to
the attacks of the nomad tribes of the desert, and
gradually conforming more and more to the habits

of those tribes. To an Israelite of the tribes west of the Jordan, the title Gileadite must have conveyed a similar impression, though in a far stronger degree to that which the title Celt does to us. What the Highlands of Scotland were a century ago to the towns of the Lowlands, that, and more than that, must Gilead have been to Samaria and Jerusalem." [1]

Such a one, then, was Elijah, as he stood before Ahab. He wore no court dress; he spoke in no polished phrase; but, like a sturdy Quaker, he refused to give any reverence, and, with his *thees* and his *thous*, his faithful warnings and his awful threatenings, he struck terror into Ahab's soul. He was such stuff as iconoclasts are made of, and he combined in himself many of the distinctive excellencies of the chief reformers of the sixteenth century. The courage of Luther, the plainness of speech of Latimer, the devoutness of Calvin, and the "perfervid" impetuosity of Knox, were all united in the character of this man of God. Yet was he " a man subject to like passions as we are." [2] There were deep springs of tenderness in his soul, and there were shadows of weakness cast even by the greatness of his strength. Still, take him for all in all, he stands alone among the prophets, overtopping them all in the rough vigour of his manhood and the unflinching courage which his faith in God inspired.

But now let us look at his first utterance before Israel's king. Every clause of it is significant, and as each came out, it must have cut keenly into Ahab's

---

[1] Smith's " Dictionary of the Bible ; " article *Elijah*.
[2] James v. 17.

soul. " As Jehovah the God of Israel liveth." This
is an oath, and in the mouths of many men it would
have been simply and only profane ; but Elijah is
very far from taking the name of the Lord in vain.
His words had a peculiar appropriateness to the
circumstances of the hour. " Jehovah liveth." Ahab
was a worshipper of Baal, the abstract representative
of power, an impersonal attribute, a blind principle ;
and, in opposition to all that, Elijah declares that
" Jehovah liveth," ay, and that he liveth as "the God
of Israel." The king had repudiated the covenant
which the Lord had made with Israel. He had
chosen to affirm that there was no Jehovah, and, by
consequence, that there was no covenant ; and now
Elijah, in the first words he utters, gives the flattest
contradiction to all these notions : " Jehovah the
God of Israel liveth ; " " Before whom I stand "—
here is another statement of the personality of God.
It is not only that Jehovah exists in some far-away
corner of the universe, where He takes no interest in
the affairs of men or in the operations of nature, so
called, but that He is here, and that I am now in His
presence, delivering His message, sustained by His
strength, and protected by His power. He has sent
me hither ; He is with me here ; He will accompany
me hence. Think not, therefore, to follow me with
thy spying minions ; dream not of putting me to
death by force or stratagem. I stand before Jehovah,
and I wear a charmed life until my work is done."
" As Jehovah liveth, there shall not be dew nor rain
these years but according to my word." He thus
perils the proof of the existence of God and of His
covenant relationship to Israel on the coming of

drought and its continuance, until he spoke the word
for the return of rain. It was a terrible judgment
which he thus denounced ; but it was one that would
come home to every inhabitant of the land, and
would prepare every heart for yielding to the truth
that the providence of Jehovah extends to all the
operations of nature and all the events of history,
and thus would strike at the very root of that idolatry
which had become so dominant among them. Ahab
believed in Baal and Ashtaroth, which, in the very
loftiest view that could be entertained regarding
them, were an ideal representation of the productive powers of nature ; but Elijah would show him,
and his people with him, that those powers which
Baal symbolised were effective only through the personal operation of Jehovah. . God would for the time
withhold His hand, to let them see that it was by His
constant agency that the dew and the rain did come;
and thus He would teach them to confide in Himself
as the personal, living, loving Jehovah, "who up-
holdeth all things by the word of His power," who is
above all, and over all, and in all. By a terrible
privation He would teach them the doctrine which
Jesus sought to impress upon His hearers by His
loving words: that Jehovah is the director of all
things, great or small; that a sparrow cannot fall
to the ground, or a rain-drop descend from the
clouds, or a globule of dew form upon a blade of
grass, without Him ; and so He would lead them
from the worship of mere external force in the
material universe to affectionate trust in the Divine
Father. By miracle, in the sense of a break-in upon
the regularity of nature, he would lead them up to

the perception of that continuous miracle, that constant agency of the personal God, by which even the ordinary processes of nature are carried on. Thus the question in dispute between Elijah on the one hand, and Ahab on the other, was the same as that which is in many quarters in debate to-day. It was the personal existence of Jehovah and His covenant relation to His own people, as opposed to that cold materialism which refuses to recognise anything but force, or law, or power, and which repudiates all special providence. In the name of the living as against the lifeless ; in the name of the personal as opposed to the impersonal ; in the name of the loving Father as distinguished from inexorable and impassive law, Elijah proclaims that there should be neither dew nor rain, and he hinges the truth of his assertions as to Jehovah on the fulfilment of his prophecy. Let the present generation give good heed to the result ! For the Lord God of Elijah liveth yet, and He will not be mocked or repudiated with impunity. Men slight the Old-Testament Scriptures, and when we preach to them from these ancient records, they sneeringly bid us remember that we are living in the nineteenth century ; but lo ! in these venerable annals we find "the interpretation of modern facts," and the antidote to modern errors. The naturalistic philosophy of to-day, which makes so much of laws and forces, and refuses to acknowledge God, is but a variety of the Baalism of Ahab; and it, too, will find its Elijah to repeat its demolition.

But now, leaving the prophet to the guidance of Jehovah as he passes out from the presence of Ahab, let us linger a few minutes longer to gather up one or two practical lessons from the history which we have thus rapidly reviewed.

Let us remark, in the first place, how insidious is the growth of sin, whether it be in the heart of an individual or in the history of a nation. Behold the idolatry of Israel, full-fledged and unblushing, in the Baalism of Ahab. But how did it begin? Away back in the time of the Judges, there was an Israelite, named Micah, who engaged a wandering Levite to become his priest, and set up a private chapel in his house, with images, and an ephod, and all the accessories of worship. When the Danites came to spy out the land, that they might chose a place in which to colonise, they visited Micah, and got his Levite to consult his oracle for them; and then, some months after, when a whole company of emigrants went from the South, they took this priest and his images with them, and carried them away to Dan.[1] Thus the people of that city became accustomed to image-worship; and so, when Jeroboam revolted from Solomon's son, and desired to set up separate religious centres for his subjects, he chose Dan for one of them.

For sixty years that state of things had existed, and the ten tribes had repaired to Bethel and to Dan, instead of going, as formerly, to Jerusalem. But the change of ritual wrought a disastrous change in the people. It weakened their spiritual perception; it lowered their moral tone; it deadened their consciences. Hence, they were just in a condition to be drawn away by the gorgeous worship and licentious and immoral rites of Baal and Ashtaroth, and

---

[1] Judges xvii., xviii.

so they fell an easy prey to Ahab's schemes. That which their fathers would have strenuously opposed, in the days of Jeroboam, they meekly accepted in the days of Ahab. But it is ever so. The nature of evil is to increase. Hence, alike as individuals, as congregations, and as communities, we should withstand the beginnings of iniquity. Indulgence in one sin blunts the conscience, and prepares the way for another which at first would have been sternly resisted, and that, in its turn, makes the soul ready for yet another. "A little leaven leaveneth the whole lump." The admission of one sin into the heart is like the reception of the Grecian horse into the Trojan city. It brings with it the germs of many more. Its name is "Gad"—a troop cometh. One evil tolerated in a church will soon generate many others. One disreputable thing permitted or sanctioned in the state will speedily produce a numerous progeny. All sins are near akin, and wherever one enters, communication is opened with all the rest. The little divergence from rectitude which is begun as a policy, because it seems to be required for some important end, will, by and by, develop into more heinous iniquity. So, if we would preserve ourselves from yielding homage to Baal, we must resist the worship of the golden calf. Mammonism prepares the way for materialism. The deification of worldly success by our mercantile Jeroboams leads on to the worship of law by our philosophic Ahabs. This was the course of things in ancient Israel; and he who cares to look around him may see the same leaven working at this hour.

Let us observe, in the second place, how, when

God has a work to do, He finds a fitting agent to do it. If all men were alike, there could be no special adaptation in any man for a particular work ; ·and no one individual could have the power of moulding or influencing his age by his intellectual or spiritual force. On the other hand, since men are not thus alike, if there were no superintending Providence, the right man might not always come at the right time, or be sent to the right place. As Wilberforce has said, "A great poet might be produced when a great general was wanted, or a wonderful financier might be given to a horde of savages."[1] But there are no such mistakes made in the providence of God. When the hour strikes, the man is ready, ay, even though it may have taken many years to fit him for the work. Elijah was prepared when it was time for him to appear. When the Gospel was to be given to the Gentiles, Paul, whose whole early training had been an unconscious preparation for his special mission, was called for the purpose ; and when the fulness of the time had come, Luther, already fitted for the work by his experiences, sprung up to nail his theses to the church-door of Wittenberg, and challenge Rome to do her worst. Nor is this all. The man who has the work to do is the right man to do it. Had Elijah been one who wore soft raiment and dwelt in kings' palaces, he could not have roused Israel as he did. Had John the Baptist been be-gloved and fashionable, dealing in silken speech and soft attire, he would never have stirred the men of his generation to repentance. His mission, like that

---

[1] "Heroes of Hebrew Monarchy," p. 319.

of Elijah, needed a fearless, blunt, undaunted man, who was not afraid to call things by their common names, and such a man God made him in the desert. We often hear slighting remarks on the great Reformers, as if they had been too stern and rugged in their bearing ; and Knox especially has hardly been forgiven by the readers of Romance because he made Queen Mary weep.   But in their days men had stern work to do, and a woman's tears are not so costly as a nation's blood.   We had not been as we are to-day if it had not been for their sternness. True, their manner would not have suited our age; but they were not sent to our age; and they were made, not only for their work, but by it.   God needs His Luthers as well as His Melancthons ; His Pauls as well as His Johns; His Latimers as well as His Leightons ; and we may as well find fault with the sweet-briar in the hedge because it is prickly, and because it is not the violet in the garden border, as complain because God's people in one age and in one department of His work are not so polished and refined as those in another.   The carpenter has tools of various fineness and with different edge. The plane would be as useless for felling trees as the axe would be for smoothing the surface of some valued piece of wood.   Each is best for its own work ; and so in the great providential and gracious work of the advancement of God's Church, each agent is most admirable for the work he does. Instead, therefore, of criticising the harshness of the Reformers, let us endeavour to find out what our particular mission is, and let us give ourselves to that with all our might.

Finally, let no one be deterred from doing what he believes to be his duty because he is alone. As we shall see, up to the time when Elisha was called, Elijah was for the most part without any coadjutor. He dwelt apart. He stood by himself. Yet God was with him and he did valiantly. Had he waited until he could persuade some fellow-man to go with him into Ahab's palace, I do not think that he ever would have entered it. But he went in God's strength, and he spoke his message with all boldness. Let no one be dismayed, therefore, because he is only one; for one man with God in him and with him is "multitudinous above all human majorities," and will and must succeed. Not that the might is in himself—he is only one—but he furnishes a medium through which the might of God, which is omnipotence, may come in contact with the evils of his age. Thus he is "mighty through God to the pulling-down of the strongholds" of iniquity. If, therefore, there be any stirrings in any one to-night towards the doing of some needful work, let him not wait for some fellow-man to accompany him; but let him go forth to it himself alone, taking with him this gracious promise: "One man of you shall chase a thousand, for the Lord your God, He it is that fighteth for you, as He hath promised you."

II.

BY THE BROOK.

1 KINGS xvii. 2-6.

HAVING delivered his startling message in the audience of Ahab, Elijah left the royal presence as abruptly as he had at first appeared. We have no record of what occurred after his departure, between the monarch and his courtiers; but we may suppose that though for the moment they were awed into solemn silence by the prophet's weird aspect and dreadful words, they would, at his exit, break out into a shout of laughter at the whole affair; for it is the manner of such men to pass from the extreme of terror to that of derision. The first emotion of the king was, perhaps, that of indignation, forming itself into the purpose to thrust Elijah into the dungeon, as, in after-days, he did with Micaiah;[1] but the rapid movement of the prophet rendered any such design abortive; and so, baffled in his intended vengeance, he would affect to look upon the whole thing with contempt. "Tush!" he might say; "'tis but some maniac who has broken loose," and in a few days the occurrence would be forgotten. But when the rainy

---

[1] 1 Kings xxii. 26, 27.

season came, and the sky above continued cloudless, blazing like burnished brass with the red glare of the fiery sun; when, month after month, no dew-drop sparkled on the withered grass; when the fountains refused to flow, and the rivers dried up in their beds, and grim, gaunt Famine began his desolating march across the land; then Ahab and his court would think upon the Tishbite, and recall his awful words.

At first, indeed, there might be little feeling of alarm, for hope is ever strong in human breasts. Though the rain was long in coming, the people would still expect it in its season, and now and again some aged man would calm their rising fears by telling them of some similar occurrence in his younger days, when, after all, the rain came at as late a date as that, and the harvest was as good as usual. But when the whole rainy season had gone by, and no right shower had fallen to refresh the thirsty land; when the grass had become blackened and destroyed, as if some prairie-fire had passed over it with its scorching breath, then the cry awoke in the palace, and was echoed in every quarter of the land, "Where is Elijah the Tishbite?" They sought him east and west, and north and south; they sought him in the towns and in the desert, on the mountain-sides and in the lonely valleys; in Gilead and Judea, in Israel and Zidonia; yea, wherever they heard that any one answering to his description had appeared, thither Ahab sent a message,[1] in the hope that he might prove to be the prophet. But all search was vain, for the Lord had hidden him; and not until it was time for him to

---

[1] 1 Kings xviii. 10.

strike another blow, would Ahab be permitted to
look upon his face.

Even as he left the palace of the king, "the word
of the Lord came unto him, saying, Get thee hence,
and turn thee eastward, and hide thyself by the brook
Cherith, that is before Jordan." It is almost impossible now to identify the locality which is here described. Three opinions have been held by scholars
regarding it. Some place it on the eastern side of
the river Jordan, and suppose that it was one of the
"Wadys" of Elijah's native Gilead. Others believe
that it was the valley of one of those brooks which
run into the Jordan from the range of hills upon its
western side ; and of those who are in favour of this
opinion some prefer the Wady Fasael, some the Wady
Kelt. This last is that which Robinson and Porter
think to be the valley of the Cherith ; and as, whether
they are correct or not, the valley in which the
prophet was concealed must have been one not unlike
the Wady Kelt, I shall quote to you the description
which Porter has given of it. "No spot in Palestine
is better fitted to afford a secure asylum to the perse-
cuted than the Wady Kelt. On each side of it extend
the bare, desolate hills of the wilderness of Judea, in
whose fastnesses David was able to bid defiance to
Saul. The Kelt is one of the wildest ravines in this
wild region. In some places it is not less than five
hundred feet deep, and just wide enough to give
passage to a streamlet like a silver thread, and to
afford space for its narrow fringe of oleanders. The
banks are almost sheer precipices of naked limestone,
and are here and there pierced with the dark open-
ings of caves and grottoes, in some one of which

Elijah may have lain concealed. It opens into the great valley ; and from its depths issues a narrow line of verdure into the white plain ; it gradually spreads as it advances, until it mingles, at the distance of a mile or more, with the thickets that encompass Riha, the modern representative of Jericho."[1]

Into this valley, or a valley like it, Elijah went. But let no one suppose that he went thither because he was afraid of any consequences that might come upon him, for the bold message which he had carried in God's name to Ahab. He went to Cherith because God sent him thither; and, in taking up his abode in his rocky cavern, he was serving his Master as faithfully as he was when he entered the palace of Jezreel to confront the king, or when he stood upon the summit of Carmel and put to shame the worshippers of Baal.

Here is a lesson which we may well take to ourselves. In this busy, bustling age, we Christians, catching somewhat the spirit of the times, are apt to imagine that God can be served only by public labour. We talk so much about "working for Christ" among the poor and ignorant and degraded, that sometimes, I fear, the sentiment of despondency is awakened by our words in the hearts of those who, by some cause or other, are for the time unable to exert themselves thus publicly in advancing the Redeemer's kingdom. But God has different departments of service, and sometimes He may send us to a place of solitude, just that we may render to Him the homage of quiet waiting and loving patience. Jesus

---

[1] Alexander's " Kitto's Encyclopædia," vol. i., p. 484.

was pleasing the Father, and advancing the great work of our salvation, as really during His forty days' sojourn in the wilderness as when He taught in the Temple courts, or preached to the multitudes upon the mountain-side. John the Baptist was "fulfilling his course" as truly when he was in the desert as after he had shown himself unto Israel. Paul was serving his Divine Master as faithfully when he was in prison as when, in Ephesus, he taught in the school room of Tyrannus; and so when, in the providence of God, we are separated from our fellowmen, either by space or by that which is just as thorough an isolater—peculiar personal experiences —let us not, therefore, imagine that we are not doing our Father's will. Not now, indeed, does Jehovah speak to us, as here He did to Elijah, and none of us may pretend that he has heard the Lord saying to him, "Go here," or "Go there;" but yet He leads us as really by His providence as He directed Elijah by His word; and when we are laid aside from active usefulness, and consigned to the solitude of a sickchamber, let us not fret ourselves with the thought that we are thereby disqualified for working for His glory. Our work, then, is to be quiet, and to manifest patience under His hand. Into such a Cherith valley, all rugged and dreary, God sent John Milton when He sealed his eyes in blindness; yet the poet was not thereby led to think that he could do nothing for his Lord. Nay, for out of the darkness of his trial he sung, like the nightingale, his song of trust and peace —after this fashion :

" When I consider how my light is spent
Ere half my days, in this dark world and wide,

And that one talent which is death to hide,
Lodged with me useless, though my soul more bent
To serve therewith my Maker, and present
My true account, lest He, returning, chide ;
' Doth God exact day labour, light denied ?'
I fondly ask. But Patience, to prevent
That murmur, soon replies : 'God doth not need
Either man's work, or His own gifts : who best
Bear His mild yoke, they serve Him best ; His state
Is kingly ; thousands at His bidding speed.
And post o'er land and ocean without rest ;
They also serve who only stand and wait.' "

Yes, thou son of sanctified genius, we thank thee
for the words, " They also serve who only stand and
wait." Whosoever thou art, therefore, whom God
has sent into some lonely Cherith, take to thyself the
comfort of these noble lines. Wait; and as thou
waitest, drink of the brook that is purling at thy feet ;
for though thou canst not do much now, thy waiting
will discipline thee, and so prepare thee to do more
hereafter.

Thus, at least, it was with Elijah here ; for we may
not cut off this period of his history from that by
which it was succeeded, and we must believe that he
was fitted, in a large measure, for his after-work by
the meditations and devotions to which he gave himself in this solitary place. It is in secret that God
performs His mightiest works. No eye has looked
into the great laboratory of Nature, wherein are mingled those elements that go to produce the effects
which are constantly appearing ; and it is in solitude,
away from the busy haunts of men, that Jehovah
works the greatest wonders of His grace. When Jesus
sought to open a blind man's eyes, He "led him aside

from the multitude;" and when, in the instance
before us, God conducted Elijah to this lonely valley,
be sure that He opened His servant's eyes to many
things which before had been invisible to him. We
may not err, perhaps, if we affirm of him at this time
what a living writer has said of the true poet:

> " He saw thro' life and death, through good and ill,
>   He saw thro' his own soul.
> The marvel of the everlasting will,
>   An open scroll,
>   Before him lay." [1]

In any case, we may surely declare that, in his long
sojourn in this rocky retreat, Elijah drank from
another stream than that which rippled at his feet,
even from the river of the water of life, that flows
from beneath the throne of God. He was never alone.
Everything around him talked to him of God, and
God Himself communed with his soul. Thus was he
strengthened and trained for the work that was before
him; and if we would ever succeed in doing anything
great for Christ, we must seek often to be "alone
with God." Indeed, if God through us intends to do
something signal for the glory of His name and the
good of our fellows, He will somehow contrive to have
us for a long while with Himself, that He may shape
to us distinctly the high ideal which He means us to
realise. It was thus He did with Moses and with
Paul, with Elijah and with John; and thus will He
discipline for special usefulness those whom He will
yet employ. Only let us notice this: it is not solitude alone that fits the soul for service, but solitude

---

[1] Tennyson.

filled and brightened and dispelled by fellowship with
God. The man that is alone with himself has, probably, the worst of all companions; he who is alone
with God has certainly the best; and when he joins
his fellow-men, they see on his very countenance the
reflection of the glory on which he has so long been
looking.

But let us pass on, to look at the promise which
God gave to Elijah in connection with the command
to proceed to Cherith. "And it shall be, that thou
shalt drink of the brook; and I have commanded
the ravens to feed thee there." The Master whom
Elijah served "sendeth no man a warfare on his own
charges." If He set one out on a pilgrimage, He will
put a staff into his hand, and will support him in the
way. If He call one to suffer for His sake, He will
sustain him by His grace, and cheer him by His favour.
And so in regard to temporal matters as well as
spiritual, if He require one of His children to do a
certain thing, He will provide for him those resources
which are needed for the doing of it. Hence, having
ordered Elijah to Cherith, He promises to provide for
his wants. It might be that there was no miracle
in the continuance of this mountain torrent; and,
indeed, it seems clear that there was none, for by
and by it failed; but there was the miracle of *prescience*,
in the assurance here given to Elijah, inasmuch as it
implied, on the part of Him who gave it, foreknowledge
that the brook would continue to flow long after the
others were dried up. Nor was this all: the careful
observer of the ways of Providence will not fail to
note the fact that the stream which ran so long was
in a hidden retreat where no one would think of seek-

ing for the prophet. "Whoso is wise, and will observe these things, even they shall understand the loving-kindness of the Lord." [1]

But more wonderful is the latter part of the promise: "I have commanded the ravens to feed thee there." So wonderful, indeed, is this pledge on the part of God to His servant that many have staggered at the words, and have attempted to bring another, and, to them, less improbable, meaning out of them. It happens that the term here translated "ravens" is rendered by the word "merchants" in Ezekiel xxvii. 27, and some have wished to take it in this sense here. Others, changing the vowels of the Hebrew word—which, within certain grammatical limits, they may do, if it be imperatively required, since they are not of any higher authority than that of the Masoretes in the fourth century—would take the term to be Arabs, or inhabitants of a town called Arabah, whose existence and location, however, are purely hypothetical. But neither of these opinions can be rested in for any length of time by the intelligent Bible-student; and it is not without considerable amazement that I find one of them advocated by a writer who has done so much for the illustration of the Scriptures as Dr. Kitto. Still, the term cannot here be understood as "merchants," since the site of the Cherith must have been far removed from the course usually followed by caravans or travelling companies. Neither can it mean inhabitants of Arabah, since, in accordance with all Hebrew analogy, if such people had been intended, they would have been

---

[1] Psalm cvii. 43.

called, not "Orebim," as the word is here, but
" Arabaim."

But the most serious objection to all these views
remains yet to be stated. The great purpose of God
in sending Elijah to Cherith was to conceal him for
the time from Ahab, and the people of Israel. Now,
to provide for him by merchants, or by the inhabitants
of a town, was to peril that concealment. A secret
may be safe in the keeping of one or two ; but when
it comes to be known to companies, or the people of
a city, it is sure to be divulged by some one. Especially would it be certain to leak out when, as in this
case, the personal interest of all the inhabitants of
the land seemed to be involved in its publication.
We can understand the stories told in Scottish glens of
the shelter given to the Covenanters, even by those who
did not quite agree with their principles ; for though
they ran a certain risk thereby, they did not directly
lose anything by screening them. But here the
whole nation was suffering from drought and consequent famine; and according to the statement of him
who threatened them in God's name with these calamities, they could not be removed until he again gave
the word. Hence, every inhabitant of the land had a
personal interest in discovering and making known
his retreat. To suppose, therefore, that in these
circumstances companies of merchants, or the dwellers
in a certain town, could keep the secret of it to themselves, in face of the particular reward offered for the
prophet's discovery, and the general advantages to be
reaped from his re-appearance, is to accept that which
is to me a far greater improbability than that the birds
of the air brought food to the prophet of the Lord.

No doubt it is objected that ravens were unclean
according to the law, but we may reply in the
words of Dr. Eadie : " The law did not prohibit
any one from using food that had been borne on the
back of a camel or horse, both of which were unclean
for food, according to the law.   Now, these creatures
performed for Elijah the same service that beasts of
burden did to people in ordinary circumstances.
Though God says to Elijah, 'I have commanded
the ravens to feed thee,' it is not meant that he
would in any way so affect their natural disposition
that they should bring food, and deposit it solely for
the prophet's use, but simply that Elijah should be
fed through their instrumentality; that they, following their natural habits, would bring food for their
own use, or for the support of their young, of which
Elijah could easily avail himself." [1]   Thus understood,
it is far more natural to take the word as describing
ravens, than to view it as implying human agency.
Of course, in either case, the hand of God would be
acknowledged by all parties ; but in the circumstances
of the prophet at the time, the agency of birds is
even more natural than that of men, while, as a
learned writer in Smith's " Dictionary " says, " There
is no escape from the plain meaning of the words,
occurring as they do in a passage otherwise display-
ing no tinge of the marvellous, or from the unanimity
of all the Hebrew MSS., and of all the ancient ver-
sions and Josephus." [2]

Such, then, was the promise of the Lord to Elijah :
water from the brook, and food from the ravens.

---

[1] Eadie's " Cyclopædia ; " article *Elijah*.
[2] Smith's " Dictionary ; " article *Elijah*.

"Poor enough fare," one may say : yet it was superior to that of multitudes in Israel, and it was all the prophet needed. "Having food and raiment, he had learned therewith to be content." He knew the meaning of "enough." Alas ! how few of us do ! He did not care for hoarding ; but, living a day at a time, he was content with a day's food each day. Happy ward of Providence ! more to be envied in thy simplicity than the wealthy millionaire, with his pistol beneath his pillow !

But we are anticipating; for now we turn to contemplate the prophet's obedience to the Divine command. "So he went and did according unto the word of the Lord : for he went and dwelt by the brook Cherith, that is before Jordan." Perhaps there was an effort needed on the part of the prophet to carry out this command of God's. Naturally, as I judge, he was fond of danger. I have heard a distinguished general say that he was never so cool, composed, and self-possessed anywhere as he was upon the field of battle ; and that, apart from the horrors that were inseparably connected with such a scene of strife, there was something in its stimulus and excitement which he felt to be intensely exhilarating. So I conceive it was with Elijah and the great moral struggle in which he was engaged. Like the war-horse so magnificently described in the Book of Job, "he scented the battle afar off, he mocked at fear and was not affrighted, neither turned he back from the sword. He saith among the trumpets, Ha, ha !"[1] He was in his congenial element when he

---

[1] Job xxxix. 22-25.

was in the thick of the spiritual conflict which God had commanded him to inaugurate and carry on ; and so it would be a trial to him to tell him to go into seclusion, especially since it might leave him open to be misjudged by his fellows. He might have been inclined to say with Nehemiah, on a memorable occasion, " Should such a man as I flee ? "[1] But God's word must not be gainsaid, and so he stood not to ask, " What will they say of me in Jezreel and throughout Israel? " or, " Could not I be engaged elsewhere in some active work ? " Neither did he inquire, in hesitating unbelief, " How will the brook be maintained ? " or " What certainty have I that the ravens will feed me ? " or, " How can I prepare the food they bring to me ? " He asked no questions. His was not " to make reply," his was not " to reason why." God had spoken : that was sufficient ; and he went his way up that lonely valley, trusting in God as truly as he did when he entered into Ahab's presence. Brethren, let us imitate Elijah here ! We may not be called to bear witness for God before princes, and may have no occasion to clothe ourselves with the thunder of His power ; but we may be called, yea, I doubt not some of us have often been already called, to go into circumstances of privation, and to trust to God's promises for our temporal support. Let us do so as implicitly as did the Tishbite here. Let us rest assured that if we love the Lord, and are in circumstances of necessity, He will take care of us, and make provision for us. Let us wait on Him in earnest

---

[1] Nehemiah vi. 11.

prayer for this very thing; for as we listen to the purling of Cherith's brook, and see the heavy flight of the raven across the valley with its supply for the prophet, we seem to hear again the words of ancient promise : " The Lord will provide." " Thy bread shall be given thee, and thy water shall be sure." " Trust in the Lord, and do good ; so shalt thou dwell in the land, and verily thou shalt be fed." " Seek first the kingdom of God and His righteousness, and all these things shall be added unto you." For the prophet, leaning upon God, was not put to shame. Jehovah stood to His word, and " the ravens brought him bread and flesh in the morning, and bread and flesh in the evening, and he drank of the brook." Everything was as God had told him. " Hath He said it, and shall He not do it ? hath He spoken, and shall He not make it good ? " " He is faithful who hath promised." But " the Lord God of Elijah " liveth yet, and is as faithful to His word as He ever was. He will keep His promises in regard to spiritual matters ; and when His people are in a land of drought and famine, then, in His own Son, He gives them bread and flesh to eat, and in His Word there is a perennial fountain from which they may always drink.

But we must not forget that He is faithful also to His promises as to temporal things. We are apt, indeed, to think that food and raiment, and other such material blessings, are too secular and small to trouble Him with, and so we all too seldom tell Him about our temporal difficulties. That is a great mistake. He wishes us to be without anxiety. He encourages us to go to Him with every care, and He assures us that either He will remove the cause of our perplexity, or strengthen us under it, to glorify His name. More frequently than we wot of does He supply His people's wants, even yet in ways apparently as extraordinary as that by which He provided for Elijah. Let me tell you of one or two. The good Krummacher, in commenting on this very passage, relates the following incident, as one well known to all his hearers:[1] "Who else was it," says he, "but the God of Elijah, who, only a short time ago, in our neighbourhood, so kindly delivered a poor man out of his distress, not, indeed, by a raven, but by a poor singing-bird. You are acquainted with the circumstance. The man was sitting, early in the morning, at his own house door; his eyes were red with weeping, and his heart cried to heaven, for he was expecting an officer to come and distrain him for a small debt. And while sitting thus with a heavy heart, a little bird flew through the street, fluttering up and down, as if in distress, until at length, quick as an arrow, it darted over the good man's head into his cottage, and perched itself on an empty cupboard. The good man, who little imagined who had sent him the bird, closed the door, caught the bird, and placed it in a cage, where it immediately began to sing very sweetly; and it seemed to the man as if it were the tune of a favourite hymn, 'Fear thou not when darkness reigns;' and as he listened to it, he found it soothe and comfort his mind. Suddenly some one knocked at the door. 'Ah! it is the officer,' thought the man, and was sore afraid. But no; it was the

---

[1] Krummacher's "Elijah the Tishbite," on this passage.

servant of a respectable lady, who said that the neighbours had seen a bird fly into his house, and she wished to know if he had caught it. 'Oh yes!' answered the man, 'and here it is;' and the bird was carried away. A few minutes after the servant came again. 'You have done my mistress a great service,' said he. 'She sets a high value upon the bird, which had escaped from her. She is much obliged to you, and requests you to accept this trifle, with her thanks.' The poor man received it thankfully, and it proved to be neither more nor less than the sum he owed. So, when the officer came, he said, 'Here is the amount of the debt. Now leave me in peace, for God has sent it me.'"

Take this other, which is intimately associated with the history of a beautiful German hymn : About two years after the close of the Thirty Years' War in Germany, George Neumarck lived in a poor street in Hamburg. Obtaining a precarious livelihood by playing on the violoncello, after a while he fell sick, and was unable to go his usual rounds. As this was his only means of support, he was soon reduced to great straits, and was compelled to part with his instrument to a Jew, who, with characteristic sharpness, lent him on it a sum much below its value for two weeks, after which, if it were not redeemed, it was to be forfeited. As he gave it up, he looked lovingly at it, and tearfully asked the Jew if he might play one more tune upon it. "You don't know," he said, "how hard it is to part with it. For ten years it has been my companion ; if I had nothing else, I had it ; and it spoke to me, and sung back to me. Of all

the sad hearts that have left your door, there has
been none so sad as mine." His voice grew thick;
then, pausing for a moment, he seized the instrument
and commenced a tune so exquisitely soft that even
the Jew listened, in spite of himself. A few more
strains, and he sung, to his own melody, two stanzas
of his own hymn, " Life is weary ; Saviour, take me."
Suddenly the key changed; a few bars, and the
melody poured forth itself anew, and his face lighted
up with a smile as he sung, " Yet who knows the cross
is precious." Then, laying down the instrument, he
said, " As God will, I am still," and rushed from the
shop. Going out into the darkness, he stumbled
against a stranger, who seemed to have been listening
at the door, and who said to him, " Could you tell
me where I could obtain a copy of that song? I
would willingly give a florin for it." " My good
friend," said Neumarck, " I will give it you without
the florin." The stranger was valet to the Swedish
ambassador, and to him the poet told the story of his
trials. He, in his turn, told his master, who, being
in want of a private secretary, engaged Neumarck at
once, and so his troubles ended. But with his first
money he redeemed his instrument, and, on obtaining
it, he called his landlady and his friends and neighbours, to hear him play on it again. Soon his room
was filled, and he sung, to his own accompaniment,
his own sweet hymn, of which this is one stanza :

" Leave God to order all thy ways,
    And hope in Him, whate'er betide ;
Thou'lt find Him, in the evil days,
    Thine all-sufficient strength and guide.

Who trusts in God's unchanging love
Builds on the rock that naught can move." [1]

But what need I more ? If it were lawful for me to bring out narratives which I have received in confidence from some whom I have visited in their distress, I could unfold illustrations, equally striking, of the great truth that God careth even for His people's temporal wants. So let our parting word for this evening be, "Trust in the Lord, and do good ; so shalt thou dwell in the land, and verily thou shalt be fed."

---

[1] See "Lives and Deeds Worth Knowing About," by Rev. W. F. Stevenson, p. 132; also "Evenings with the Sacred Poets," by Frederick Saunders, pp. 177-179.

III.

THE BARREL AND THE CRUSE.

1 KINGS xvii. 7–16.

HOW long Elijah dwelt in the valley of the Cherith we are not precisely informed; for the phrase "after a while," even if we adopt the more literal rendering in the margin, "at the end of days," is quite indefinite, and furnishes no data on which we can found any opinion. We may, perhaps, conjecture that he remained in his retreat for a period not shorter than four or five months, and not longer than a year; and in any case, during the later portion of his sojourn, his faith must have been put to a very severe test, "for the brook began to fail." Each day, therefore, he would mark that the waters had receded, and laid bare another portion of the shingly channel over which they flowed, until at length he might require to make little artificial pools, into which, after a time, a proper supply might percolate. In such circumstances, if his faith had not been securely fixed in God, his heart might have failed just as the brook declined; and even with his strong confidence in Jehovah, the receding rivulet must have had a saddening influence upon his spirit. Sight does and must affect us more or less, so long as we are in the body, and sight here must have done much to depress Elijah. He was like one immured in that terrible dungeon which the cruelty of the Inquisition devised, and which gradually, day by day, narrowed in upon its victim, crushing him at last in its fatal embrace. He was like the man whom John Foster has so graphically described in one of his lectures, who had only a certain supply of water in a cistern, and who, each time he took a draught therefrom, felt that he was lessening the resources of his life. Here was the brook drying up, until there was nothing left but a little rippling thread. What was he to do when it should be entirely gone?

It is impossible to conceive that this question would not force itself into his thoughts, and ever as it came, there would be a fight between faith and sight. Nor let any one suppose that the ordeal was not severe, for, as John Kitto has well remarked, "it is such slow processes that try faith most of all. Many possess the faith for sudden great heroic deeds, for one who can maintain his faith unshaken in the midst of such slow trials as this." [1] But Elijah stood the test. God had sent him to Cherith ; and until God sent him elsewhere, he would remain there, sure that he would somehow be supported. Be it that the brook failed, was not God still his God? and could not He provide for him as easily without the brook as with it? So he would stay till God should bid him thence. This is the highest form of obedience—to remain at our post, even though we may be unable to see why we are kept there, and may

[1] "Daily Bible Illustrations," vol. iv., p. 241.

have to endure considerable hardship while we continue there. It is told of General Havelock's son,
that one day his father, having some business to do
in the neighbourhood, left him on London Bridge,
and bid him await his return there. Having finished
his business, which required longer time than he had
calculated, the general remembered another engage-
ment for which he was then due, and, forgetting his
son, pushed on to keep his appointment. Thus it
was with him all through the afternoon, and he
reached his home about eight o'clock in the evening.
As he was putting on his slippers, his wife said to
him, "Where's Harry?" "Dear me!" said he, "I
quite forgot; he is on London Bridge, and has been
there for the last eight hours. I must go and relieve
him." So, putting on his boots again, he hastened to
the bridge, and there he found his son pacing to and
fro, like a sentinel, along its pavement. Now, why
is it that we admire such conduct as that of the
young soldier in such a case? Why is it that our
hearts thrill, and our eyes moisten, as we read Mrs.
Hemans's well-known lines on the noble Casabianca?
Is it not because we see in them both the highest
form of obedience—that which can wait through
suffering, and, it may be, also through death, at the
post of duty, even if there be no clear comprehension
of the reason why such delay is required? Now, it
was quite similar with Elijah here. God had spoken;
and till God should speak again, he would abide
where he was, no matter though the brook was failing.
The Israelites in the desert moved when the pillar of
cloud moved and went before them; and when it
rested, they rested. To Elijah's view, the cloud was

still resting in the valley of the Cherith, and not until it rose and led him elsewhere would he leave his lonely cave.

At length, however, the word of the Lord came to him, and came in such a form as to furnish a new trial to his faith; for it said, "Arise, get thee to Zarephath, which belongeth to Zidon, and dwell there: behold, I have commanded a widow woman there to sustain thee." Now, obedience to this command required that he should cross the entire tract of Israel lying between Jordan and the coast of the Mediterranean Sea; that he should go to the territory of Eth-baal, the idolatrous father of the vindictive Jezebel; and that even there he should be cast upon the support of a woman, whose natural bread-winner and protector had been stricken from her side. It did not seem a very inviting prospect; but it was God that gave him the command, and so "he arose and went to Zarephath." We have no account of his journeyings across the country. Probably they were performed at night, when he could hope to keep himself hidden from the people's view; certainly, they were done in secret; and so far from thrusting himself into the busy haunts of men, he would seek the solitude of the most hidden paths.

The town of Zarephath was situated on the sea-coast, between Tyre and Sidon, but rather nearer the latter than the former. Its modern representative is Surafend, which seems, however, according to Dr. Thomson,[1] to have been built after the twelfth century, since at the time of the Crusaders the city stood

---

[1] "The Land and the Book," p. 161.

upon the shore. Dean Stanley[1] thus writes regarding it : " The identity of Surafend with Sarepta is
unquestioned. It is a village seated aloft on the top
and side of one of the hills, the long lines of which
skirt the plain of Phœnicia, conspicuous from afar by
the white domes of its many tombs of Mussulman
saints. It throws no light on the story of Elijah, beyond the emphasis imparted to his visit by the complete separation of the situation from the Israelite
territory on the other side of the hills."

The fact that the prophet was sent out of the land
of Israel has thus been commented on by our Lord,
in His address in the synagogue at Nazareth : "I tell
you of a truth, many widows were in Israel in the
days of Elias, when the heaven was shut up three
years and six months ; but unto none of them was
Elias sent, save unto Sarepta, a city of Sidon, unto a
woman that was a widow." [2]   Now, it has been usual
with many to look upon this as an illustration of the
divine sovereignty, and, of course, I readily admit
that God has a right to do as He pleases in the
government of the world, and in the dispensation of
His grace. I admit, also, that there are many of His
actions for which, though we are sure that He has
Himself good reason, we can give no account but this,
" Even so, Father, for so it seemeth good in Thy
sight." But this of sending Elijah to Zarephath is
not one of these ; and the Saviour, in the discourse
from which I have quoted, very clearly, as it seems
to me, unfolds the reason of the divine procedure in
the matter. You observe, He is illustrating the pro-

---

[1] " Sinai and Palestine," p. 271.　　　[2] Luke iv. 25, 26.

verb that "A prophet is not accepted in his own country."[1] Let us look, therefore, at the whole history in the light of these words. Israel had cast off allegiance to God. There were still a few, indeed, who had never bowed the knee to Baal, but the vast majority of the people had broken the divine covenant. They would have none of God, or of His prophet. Therefore God, when He had the special blessing of deliverance in time of famine to confer, would not bestow it upon any of them. He would give it to a Zidonian widow, to teach the Israelites of that day that, if they forsook God, He would forsake them, and to forewarn the Jews of after-generations that if they rejected the mercy of God, He would pass them by, and give salvation to the Gentiles. Now, the point of the reference made to this incident by Jesus lies in this : the men of Nazareth rejected Him; they said, " Is not this Joseph's son ? " and He, by recalling the two memorable passages in the history of Elijah and Elisha, plainly indicates that for their rejection they would be passed by, and that the blessing which they had despised would be handed over, first, to other portions of Israel, and then to the Gentiles ; and it was their perception of this that so enraged the men of Nazareth that they took the Lord, and led Him " to the brow of the hill whereon their city was built, that they might cast him down headlong."[2]

Thus the mission of Elijah to Zarephath was not merely an act of punishment to the Israelites of his day, because they had rejected God, but it

---

[1] Luke iv. 24.   [2] Ibid., iv. 29.

was a historical prophecy of the calling of the Gentiles consequent upon the rejection of the Gospel by the Jews, and the rejection of the Jews by the Lord. It is a solemn thing to undervalue either the Gospel or its messengers. The Gospel shall not cease to bless, and the messengers shall not cease to proclaim it; but the blessing shall descend on other lands, and the message shall be proclaimed in other ears. Therefore, if we would not forfeit the high privileges which God has conferred upon us, it becomes us to value and improve them to the uttermost.

If it be asked, again, why, of all the inhabitants of Zarephath, Elijah was sent to a poor widow, then I answer that, had he gone to some of the great ones of the place, he could not so readily have kept himself concealed from the knowledge of the authorities of the land; while, again, it was the design of God that he should sojourn with some one whom he could benefit, and for whose sake the divine power might be signally manifested. Nor is this all. There might be some feeling after the Lord of Israel in the heart of the poor woman herself; for she says to Elijah, "The Lord thy God," and she seems to have had faith enough to grasp at once the promise which the prophet repeated in His name. I know not, indeed, that she was a real heart-worshipper of the true God, but these things seem to indicate that her face was in the right direction; and so, on the principle of the promise that "to him that hath shall more be given," this poor woman, who had so much knowledge of Jehovah, was to get more. Just as to Cornelius, the devout man, Peter was sent to help him on to Christianity, so, perhaps, to this woman Elijah was sent to perfect her in the knowledge of Jehovah. God says, "I have commanded a widow woman there to sustain thee." This does not mean that the word of the Lord came to her as it did to Elijah himself, but simply, as we explained a similar mode of speech in the case of the ravens, that God would sustain the prophet through her instrumentality. In the course of Divine providence Elijah would be supported by a widow in Zarephath.

But how was he to know to which of all the widows of the city he was sent? It does not appear that any information was given him on this point until he reached the gate of the town ; but as he approached the entrance into the city, he saw a woman gathering sticks, and (guided, as I doubt not, by the suggestion of the Holy Spirit) he made up to her, and asked if she would kindly " fetch him a little water in a vessel, that he might drink." He had walked probably a long way ; it was a time of drought, and he was exhausted with his journey. It was natural, therefore, that he should make such a request. But water was a scarce commodity just then, and the woman might have been excused by many if she had declined to comply with the wishes of a stranger. Still she went to do as he had asked ; but, while she was going, he called after her and said, "Bring me, I pray thee, a morsel of bread in thine hand." This, however, seemed almost more than she could bear ; so she made reply, revealing a terrible depth of distress by her words : "As the Lord thy God liveth, I have not a cake, but a handful of meal in a barrel, and a little oil in a cruse : and, behold, I am gathering two sticks that I may go in and dress it for me and my son, that we may eat it and die." Here, indeed, is extremity

of misery. "Surely," might the prophet have said,
"this is not she to whom I am sent;" but he did
not say that. He saw in her the very person for
whose deliverance he had so opportunely come. So
he said to her, "Fear not; go and do as thou hast
said: but make me thereof a little cake first, and
bring it unto me, and after that make for thee and for
thy son. For thus saith the Lord God of Israel, The
barrel of meal shall not waste, neither shall the cruse
of oil fail, until the day that the Lord sendeth rain
upon the earth." "Make me thereof a little cake
first;" as the woman heard these words she might
be disposed to say, "Well, you are amazingly cool!
Here have I left only a meal for myself and my son;
and you, an entire stranger to us both, have the face
to ask that I should make a cake for you before I do
anything for ourselves." Truly Bishop Hall is right
when he says, "Some sharp dame would have taken
up the prophet, and have sent him away with an empty
repulse: 'Bold Israelite, there is no reason in this
request. Wert thou a friend or a brother even,
with what face couldst thou require to pull my last bite
out of my mouth.'"[1] But the promise with which
the prophet closed his petition wiped out any apparent
impertinence in the supplication itself. It was a matter
of reciprocity. Elijah said, virtually, "If you make me
this cake according to my entreaty, God will give you
all through this terrible drought the material to make
as many cakes as you need." And, believing in
God's ability and willingness to keep His promise, she

[1] "Contemplations on the Historical Passages of the Old
and New Testaments," by the Right Rev. Joseph Hall, D.D.,
p. 281.

closed at once with the prophet's offer, and went and
did as he had said. And God kept His word ; for
" the barrel of meal wasted not, neither did the cruse
of oil fail, according to the word of the Lord which
He spake by Elijah."

Now here let us pause, and glean for ourselves a
few lessons from this touching narrative.

The first thing that strikes us is the minuteness of
God's daily providence. We knew before that God
cares for all things, and especially for His own children, but having read attentively over this portion of
His Word, and having studied it in all its bearings, we
see that truth set in a clearer light than we commonly
behold it. The Redeemer Himself has said that " a
sparrow cannot fall to the ground without our Father; "
but, somehow, as we read His words, the very mag-
nitude of the truth which they convey staggers our
intellects ; and it is only when we have it exemplified
in a case like that before us, that we thoroughly
understand all that it implies. Behold at what subtle
points, all unknown to ourselves, our histories touch
each other ; and how, by the prearrangements of
God's care, He works out His purposes of mercy,
even through the agency of our own free wills ! This
woman had no thought of meeting God's prophet at
the gate of Zarephath. She went out with a sad
heart to gather fuel for her last meal, and, lo ! she
meets one who was destined to turn her mourning
into gladness. Nor is this a solitary instance. The
woman of Samaria, going out for her daily supply of
water, meets the Lord, who bestows upon her salvation. The two disciples go to find a place wherein
to eat the passover, and they meet a man with a

pitcher of water, whose only thought was to take home that which was needed for his family's wants. A similar thing happened when other two went for the colt whereon Jesus rode into Jerusalem. Lydia finds her way to the Jewish place of prayer by the riverside in the outskirts of Philippi, thinking, no doubt, of the God of Israel, and the privileges of the people of His choice, and lo ! Paul is there, and listening to his word, she is converted to the Lord. But this minute providence is not confined to the ages of which we read in Holy Writ. It is the same still. Scoffing men call its manifestations mere coincidences; but it is as true now as it ever was, that God is in all, and over all, and through all things. He is "not far from every one of us." He is on every side of us. His providence encircles us with His protection, and guides us by His wisdom, albeit at the moment we feel only that we are doing according to our choice. What a comfort there is in the assurances that God is with us and that God is for us, so that each of us can sing with David, " I am poor and needy, yet the Lord thinketh upon me."

But, in the second place, we learn here that, no matter how small our resources may be, we can still do something for God, if we have but the will. This poor woman could scarcely have been in more destitute circumstances. She was at the point of starvation, and yet, by her unselfish liberality with what she had, she was honoured of God to sustain His prophet for, perhaps, two years. But have we not seen similar things often in the history of God and of His Church? No matter how feeble the instrument we use, when God is behind it He can make it mighty.

An ox-goad in the hand of Shamgar; a bone in the
hand of Samson ; lamps, pitchers, and trumpets in the
hands of Gideon's three hundred ; a sling and a stone
in the hand of David, have all done great things in
overthrowing God's enemies. A few loaves and fishes
put by a lad into the Saviour's hand have fed thousands on the mountain-side. And it is so still. I
read some years ago, in the *Sunday Magazine,* of a
common milk-man, who, out of his own earnings,
bought a house, in which he sustained and educated
and trained to some useful trade a dozen orphans
picked off the streets of London. He began with the
little that he had, and God opened up his way before
him to that, for him, great result. Let no one, therefore, be discouraged, or say that he can do nothing.
A few drops of water rightly utilised by the hydraulic
crane may lift the heaviest weights, and the scantiest
resources, if there be but faith and resolution, may
work wonders in the world. Admirably here has
Macduff remarked : " It is worthy of note that this
power of littles is specially illustrated in Holy Writ in
connection with two widows, the one in the Old
Testament and the other in the New. The widow of
Sarepta giving the last handful in her drained barrel
the widow at the Temple treasury casting in her two
mites. Never let any one say, ' I am of no use in
the world ; I can do no good ; I can exercise no
influence. God has clipped my wings. I am like a
chained bird. I would soar, but I cannot—this cage
of poverty and sickness so keeps me shut up from the
elements of society, activity, and usefulness.' "[1] Ah !

---

[1] " The Prophet of Fire," by J. R. Macduff, D.D., p. 61.

D

no. When God has no more for us to do here, He
will take us hence; but so long as He keeps us on
earth, He has work for us, no matter how scanty our
resources, or how feeble our power. Nay, if we will
only view it rightly, our weakness will be our strength,
so that, like Paul, we shall say, "When I am weak,
then am I strong."

We may learn here, thirdly, that our doings for God
should go before our devotion to ourselves. The
world's maxim is, "Take care of yourself first;" the
Christian principle is to merge self in Christ. God
requires the first-fruits. It will not do merely to serve
ourselves and give the surplus to Him. We must serve
Him, and help His servants, and advance His cause,
even if we should be required, like this woman here,
to eat a smaller cake ourselves, and to give a smaller
portion to our families. There is no faith in giving
to God only what we can spare after we have served
ourselves. Faith will, like the poor widow at the
treasury, give all, if need be, to God, and look to
Him for a supply. The dying Sidney caused the water
which was brought for him to be given to a soldier
who seemed to need it more than he. There was the
true spirit of Christ, who yielded up Himself that
sinners thereby might be saved. Selfishness is the
essence of sin. Love is the essence of salvation.
The haughty Cain stands by and says, "Am I my
brother's keeper?" The meek follower of the Lord
Jesus will share his last comfort with his brethren in
wretchedness and want. This is a hard thing to the
men of the world; but when once we thoroughly
understand and appreciate what Jesus has done for
us, it becomes easy.

We may learn, fourthly, that in giving thus to God we are taking the surest means to get more from Him. He will be no man's debtor ; and what He gets from us, through His children, He repays again with an abundant increase. This woman gave one meal to the prophet, and God sustained her for two years. Christ gave Himself for sinners, and, lo ! God has exalted Him to the throne of mediatorial dominion, and is even now satisfying His heart by letting Him see of "the travail of His soul." This is ever the divine law : we get by giving. We must sow if we would reap ; we must open our hearts in love to others if we would have God's love shed abroad in our own souls. It will not do, however, for us to have regard to the reward. We are to "do good and lend, look-ing for nothing again ; " and then it is that our reward shall be great, and "we shall be the children of the Highest."

Nor is it only in the giving of supplies for the bodies of men that this principle holds good. It is as true of the labours which we engage in for their spiritual benefit. "He that watereth others, shall be watered also himself." Hence, when we find our piety at a low ebb, or our happiness diminishing, the way to increase it is to go and try to make others better and more joyous. Very beautifully has this lesson been sung for us by the authoress of "The Schonberg-cotta Family " in these lines :—

" Is thy cruse of comfort failing? Rise and share it with another,
  And through all the years of famine it shall serve thee and thy
    brother.
  Love divine will fill thy store-house, or thy handful still renew ;
  Scanty fare for one will often make a royal feast for two.

"For the heart grows rich in giving ; all its wealth is living
    grain ;
Seeds which mildew in the garner, scattered, fill with gold
    the plain.
Is thy burden hard and heavy?   Do thy steps drag wearily?
Help to bear thy brother's burden ; God will bear both it and
    thee.

"Numb and weary on the mountains, wouldst thou sleep amidst
    the snow?
Chafe that frozen form beside thee, and together both shall
    glow.
Art thou stricken in life's battle?   Many wounded round thee
    moan :
Lavish on their wounds thy balsam, and that balm shall heal
    thine own.

"Is the heart a well left empty?   None but God its void can fill ;
Nothing but a ceaseless fountain can its ceaseless longings still.
Is the heart a living power?   Self-entwined, its strength sinks
    low ;
It can only live in loving, and by serving love will grow."[1]

We may learn, fifthly, that God's doings for us are
often delayed till the very last, to teach us that, when
relief comes, it comes from Him.   Not till the brook
was quite dried up did Jehovah make provision for
Elijah ; and the widow was preparing her last meal
when Elijah came, an apparent burden to her, but
yet a real helper.   "Man's extremity is God's opportunity."   It is not till things "are at the worst" that
they "begin to mend."   Thus even the world's proverb recognises this principle of the divine procedure.
It was in the fourth watch of the night, when they
were worn out by their long toil in rowing, that Jesus

---

[1] "The Women of the Gosples, and other Poems," by the
author of "Chronicles of the Schonberg-cotta Family," p. 181.

came walking over the sea to His disciples' assistance.
It was after Lazarus had been buried that the Lord
came to help His friends at Bethany; and though
Jairus cried, "Come down, ere my child die," He let
the child expire before He went. Let us not despair,
therefore, no matter how dark may be the outlook.
"In the mount the Lord will provide," and at the
very moment of sacrifice a ram will be substituted for
our Isaac. It were a sad thing to be in perplexity
with no God to fall back upon; but while we have
Him saying to us, "I am thy God," all is well. The
deepest agony is not that of the Christian when he is
in extremity, for he knows that God is as omnipotent
then as ever, and will take care of him; but, oh! it
is sad, ineffably sad, when a man has nothing but
earthly things to sustain him. The day will come
when for him, too, the brook will fail, and the barrel
become empty; and what shall he do then without
a God? Let the godless before me ponder well the
question.

I cannot conclude without directing attention here
to God's care for the widow. He might have sent
Elijah to some other poor household; but He chose
a widow, to remind us, among other things, of His
tenderness for those who have been thus bereaved.
He is the judge of the widows. He takes them under
His peculiar care. These are His precepts to His
ancient people: "Ye shall not afflict any widow, or
fatherless child. If thou afflict them in any wise, and
they cry at all unto me, I will surely hear their cry." [1]
He commanded that sheaves should be left for them

---

[1] Exodus xxii. 22, 23.

upon the harvest-field, and gleanings from the olive-trees and from the vintage were to be reserved for them.[1] Go read anew the story of Naomi and Ruth, two widows in one home. Ponder well the teachings of this history which has been to-night before us. Think why, of all bereaved ones, Jesus chose to raise the son of the widow of Nain, and then say if we are not thereby taught to deal kindly with those who have been left to the dreariest loneliness the earth can know. And you, ye solitary ones, whom God has thus bereft of your beloved companions and pro-tectors, hear ye not again to-night these words of promise, intensified by the story of my text?—"Leave thy fatherless children, I will preserve them alive; and let thy widows trust in me."

---

[1] Deuteronomy xxiv. 19–21.

IV.

DEATH AND RESURRECTION.

1 KINGS xvii. 17-24.

ELIJAH must have sojourned with the widow of Zarephath for two years, during which he and his hostess were provided for by what seems to have been a regularly-recurring miracle. The meal in the barrel was always just on the point of being exhausted ; and the oil in the cruse was always just on the point of failing. Yet neither ever entirely gave out. There was never at any time in the house a store of either ; yet as each new day dawned, the woman discovered that she had still enough for that day's necessity. Thus while she and her guest had always a sufficiency, they were at the same time always kept on the very confines of want ; and so they were preserved from either sinking into despair or rising into presumption. God wished them both to depend directly and immediately upon Himself, and therefore He allowed no reserve to accumulate in their hands, lest they should confide in that, rather than in Him. He gave them " day by day their daily bread." And though now such miracles as that performed for the widow are no longer wrought by Him, we must neither forget nor despise the one great, constant miracle of

His providence by which His universe is sustained and His people upheld.   Is there not, in this regard, still too much ground for the appeal of the Christian poet when he says?

> " What prodigies can power divine perform
>   More grand than it produces year by year,
>   And all in sight of inattentive man?
>   Familiar with the effect, we slight the cause,
>   And in the constancy of nature's course,
>   The regular return of genial months,
>   And renovation of a faded world,
>   See naught to wonder at.   Should God again,
>   As once in Gideon, interrupt the race
>   Of the undeviating and punctual sun,
>   How would the world admire !   But speaks it less
>   An agency divine, to make him know
>   His moment when to sink and when to rise,
>   Age after age, than to arrest his course?
>   All we behold is miracle, but, seen so duly,
>   All is miracle in vain." [1]

This witness is true.   The hand that supplied our wants this morning is the same as that which provided for the widow of Zarephath and her exile guest; yet how little gratitude do we feel for this regularly-recurring kindness from the Lord, as compared with that which would thrill our souls if some miracle were wrought for our behoof!   Let us never forget, however, that what men call natural and what they call supernatural are both alike from God: only the natural represents His constant operations, the supernatural His occasional variations from His common plan.   For the one, therefore, as really as for the

---

[1] Cowper's "Task," book ii.

other, He deserves, and should receive, our loving thanks.

How Elijah was occupied during his sojourn at Zarephath does not appear; but the fact that he was, as it were, under hiding from Ahab, renders it, in a manner, certain that he was not engaged in any public effort for the spiritual benefit of the people of the place. Hence his attention must have been given almost exclusively to the duties of the closet and of the home. Much of his time would doubtless be given to devotional retirement; but he would also take the liveliest interest in his hostess and her son. His life before them would be a constant sermon, preaching to them of holiness and peace and cheerfulness, and communion with God; and it is likely that, in his conversation with the widow, he would seek to instruct her in the knowledge of Jehovah, whose personal existence, almighty power, and sovereign mercy were all so vividly made manifest in the miracle by which they were supported. I cannot help thinking, however, that the brightest feature of Elijah's life at Zarephath would be his companionship with the widow's son. We are not informed, indeed, what the age of this child was; but we think, from certain expressions in the narrative, such as those which speak of him as being in his mother's bosom, and as lifted by Elijah and carried up to his chamber, that he must have been very young. Now, knowing how interesting the prattle of an intelligent little boy is, and how much there is, even in the questions which he is continually asking, that tends both to instruct and to amuse an older mind, I feel certain that this child must have been a continuous source of delight

to the prophet; for it is a common thing for those
with stern natures like his to have a soft and tender
enjoyment in domestic life, and in fellowship with the
young. The rock which on its seaward side stands
abrupt, perpendicular, and bare, ready to meet and to
repel all the assaults of ocean, does, on its landward
side, hold out its arms to the soil, and carries on its
bosom the soft moss, the beautiful lichen, or the
blooming flower; so the reformer who, before kings
and emperors and princes, stands unbending and
unabashed, does yet at home open his heart to all the
tender affections of the family, and delights especially
in children. What can be more charming in its play-
ful *abandon*, its happy cheerfulness, its childish love
of sport, than the home-life of Martin Luther? And
they who know only the determined attitude of Knox
before Queen Mary will hardly be prepared to find
that in his home he was genial, and fond of pleasantry.[1]
So, I think, we shall do Elijah injustice if we regard
him as all rugged, hard, and cold. There were
fountains of love within him deep and fresh, and I
picture him to myself at Zarephath with this little boy
between his knees or in his arms; now amusing him
and instructing him at one and the same time with the
rehearsal of some old Hebrew story; and now, again,
in his turn, amused and instructed by the queer com-
ments which the child made upon them, and the suggestive questions which he asked regarding them. Of
course, it is a fancy; but I like to portray to myself
the Tishbite, with his hairy garment and his stern
aspect, fondling this widow's son, and telling him some

---

[1] See M'Crie's " Life of Knox," period viii.

one of those beautiful histories which have been the special favourites of children in every age and in every land. And if, as Eastern tradition declares— not very trustworthily, I admit—this boy grew up to become the prophet Jonah,[1] I can see how these early years must have been among the happiest and most profitable of his life ; and in any case, whatever his after-history, the stories of Joseph, and Moses, and Samuel, and David must have been doubly dear to him from their association with Elijah, from whose lips he had first heard them.

But in the midst of all this enjoyment, a terrible trial, severe in itself, yet rendered intensely more so from its unexpectedness, fell upon him and his hostess. "It came to pass, after these things, that the son of the woman, the mistress of the house, fell sick, and his sickness was so sore that there was no breath left in him :" that is to say, he suddenly sickened and died ; for there is no foundation whatever for the idea—which I am surprised to find countenanced by such a commentator as Lange—that he merely swooned. Death is always a sad thing, but there were here some peculiar elements of sorrow. It was the death of a child. We expect the old to die ; but our hearts cling tenderly to the young, while we almost refuse to contemplate the possibility of their being taken from us. Their winning ways, their unsophisticated simplicity, their undisguised affection, and their childish prattle endear them to our souls ; and, untaught by the experience of others, we *will* look forward to the time when they shall grow up to

[1] Stanley's "Jewish Church," vol. ii. p. 299.

help us in the business of life, and sustain us in our
old age. But their death dashes these hopes to the
ground, and robs us of the happiness which we so
highly prized. Hence, even though we have the
perfect assurance of their eternal salvation, we cannot but be filled with sadness by their removal. The
very silence of our dwelling becomes oppressive to us ;
and wherever we turn our eyes, we meet some little
plaything or some tiny shoe that is indiss)lubly
associated with the happiness of the past, so that we
cry out in anguish,

> " Dear as remembered kisses after death,
> And sweet as those by hopeless fancy feigned
> On lips that are for others ; deep as love,
> Deep as first love, and wild with all regret,
> O Death in Life—the days that are no more ! " [1]

But this boy thus unexpectedly removed was, so far
as appears, an only child. When this woman's
husband died, we may suppose that her son did something, even by his very weakness, to reconcile her to
her sorrow, and that as she clasped him to her bosom,
she would say, " Sweet, my child, I'll live for thee ; "
but now she is *alone*. There is no other little one to
stand by her knee, and draw her thoughts away from
herself, and solace her by those nameless and inde-
scribable attentions by which a child can endear
itself to a parent. Bereavement, indeed, is always
painful ; and even in a family of patriarchal size, the
absence of one will make a blank which every
member of the household will feel. Yet while others
are left, there are duties to be performed, and plans

---

[1] Tennyson's " Princess."

to be forecast; and these will not allow us to sit
down and nurse our grief. But there was no such
mitigating circumstance in this woman's condition, for
she had no other child ; and this new sorrow would
have additional bitterness, because it opened up the
old wound of her husband's death, and made it bleed
afresh.

Besides, there were certain other considerations
which gave an aspect of mystery to this dispensation.
Some time before she had looked death in the face,
and was in a manner prepared to meet it. When
Elijah first came to her, and made that singular
request to her for bread, she had no other thought
than that, after eating their last meal, she and her son
would die ; and, so far as appears, she was then stoic-
ally reconciled to her fate. But since then God had
been miraculously providing for her, day by day, and
it did seem most perplexing that, at the very moment
when He was working a miracle to save them all from
starvation, He should allow death in another form to
come upon her child. Was not this as if He were
casting down in a moment that which for months He
had been sustaining? And if this were so, why
should He have begun to sustain her at all ? Had the
blow fallen at the time when she was feeling the
famine, she could have understood it; but that it
should come now, while Jehovah was still graciously
providing for her, this was incomprehensible. Hence,
she was driven into despair. She could not understand God's dealings with her. But as the prophet
had been the instrument through whom her own life
and her son's had been preserved, she imagined that
he now must be somehow connected with the coming

of this calamity; and she went to him, crying, in
passionate grief, "What have I to do with thee, O
thou man of God? Art thou cóme unto me to call
my sin to remembrance, and to slay my son?"
That is to say, "What is there in common to us two
—to me, a sinful woman, and to thee, a man of God
—that we should thus be brought together to my
harm?" But Elijah was apparently as much amazed
and distressed as she was, and her bitter upbraidings
must have fallen painfully upon his heart. Yet he indulged in no recrimination. He saw the mother's
heart was broken, and he would not harshly judge
her for a hasty word spoken in such bewildering circumstances. He simply said, "Give me thy son;"
and, taking him out of her bosom, he carried him up
to the upper room,[1] which, as an honoured guest, he
occupied, and laid him upon his own bed. But what
did he mean by taking the dead body of the dear boy
thither? A great thought, a grand purpose, had taken
possession of his soul. Already by his prayers he had
sealed up the dew and the rain; what should hinder,

---

[1] " Our translation makes Elijah live in a loft, but not very
accurately. In Hebrew it is *'alliyeh*, and this is the common
Arabic word for the upper rooms of houses. The *'alliyeh* is the
most desirable part of the establishment, is best fitted up, and
is still given to guests who are to be treated with honour.
The women and servants live below, and their apartment is called
ardiyeh, or ground-floor, in common parlance simply *beit*, or
house. We may infer several things from this word : that the
mode of building in Elijah's time and the custom of giving the
'alliyeh to the guest were the same as now ; also, that this widow
woman was not originally among the very poorest classes, but
that her extreme destitution was owing to the famine which then
prevailed."—" The Land and the Book," p. 160.

therefore, that, by his prayers, he should raise the dead? It needed divine power to do the one ; it required no more than divine power to do the other. True, it had been heretofore unheard of in the history of the race; yet "was there any thing too hard for the Lord?" He would ask that the child might live; He would take hold of Jehovah's strength, and bring that to bear upon the distress of his hostess. "The kingdom of heaven suffereth violence ;" he would be violent, and "take it by force." So he cried, and said, "O Jehovah, my God, hast Thou also brought evil upon the widow with whom I sojourn, by slaying her son?" Then, stretching himself three times upon the child, he called upon the Lord, and said, "O Jehovah, my God, I pray Thee, let this child's soul come into him again." It was God who had inspired this desire into His servant's soul, and He granted the request, for the soul of the child came to him again, and he revived. So, descending with him to his mother's chamber, the prophet had the unspeakable satisfaction of restoring him to her embrace ; and who may attempt to describe the ecstasy of that moment in her experience, as, with every lingering suspicion banished from her mind, she said to him, "Now I know that thou art a man of God, and that the word of the Lord in thy mouth is truth"?

It is impossible for us now, with the New Testament in our hands, to read the account of this miracle without being impressed with the fact that we have here an anticipation of the Christian doctrine of the resurrection of the dead. This miracle was also a prediction. It would have been impossible to grant the prayer of Elijah here, had it not been, in the fore-

knowledge of Jehovah, an absolutely certain thing
that Jesus Christ should, in the fulness of time, die
for human offences, and rise again, not only for the
justification of believers, but also as "the first-fruits
of them that sleep." Even as the blessings which
came to the pious Israelite through his regular offering of sacrifices were pledges of the blessings which
should flow from the true and infinite atonement
which was yet to be made, so the raising again of this
dead child was a foretaste and earnest of the general
resurrection. Neither this partial and individual
resurrection in Elijah's day, nor the general resurrection at the last, could have been possible except on
the ground of the resurrection of Christ. True, in
the one case Christ's resurrection was still in the
future, and in the other it will be a long way in the
past. Yet it is alike connected with them both; and
this incident in ancient history was thus not only an
assurance that Christ should rise from the dead, but
also a prediction of the day when "all that are in
their graves shall hear the voice of the Son of man,
and shall come forth." We do not look our last
upon our believing friends, or on our beloved little
ones, when we lay their remains in the grave. We
shall see them again, and our hearts shall rejoice.
"If we believe that Jesus died, and rose again from
the dead, even so them also who sleep in jesus will
God bring with him." Then, again, the child shall
be restored to the mother, the friend to the friend,
the brother to the brother, and they shall be "for ever
with the Lord." Truly, in view of this revelation, we
may exclaim, "Our Saviour Jesus Christ, has abol-
ished death, and brought life and immortality to light

through the Gospel." Let the bereaved among us, therefore, be comforted. For good and sufficient reasons, the resurrection of our loved ones has been delayed; but it will take place, and the reunion between us will be all the sweeter because of the bitterness of the separation that has gone before.

Further, we cannot read this history, wherein the greatness of Elijah comes so prominently out, without being impressed with the peerless pre-eminence of the Lord Jesus Christ. Elijah strives after this miracle with exhaustive effort; but when Christ raises the dead, it is with infinite ease. Elijah was a servant, Christ was the Son, of God. Elijah wrought with delegated power; Christ wrought with His own might. Elijah wrought through prayer, securing thereby that Jehovah should put forth His omnipotence; Jesus wrought by commanding, in the majesty of His own inherent divinity. Elijah strained after this miracle like one, who, standing upon tiptoe, seeks to reach something that is far above him; Jesus, when He raised the widow's son, or the daughter of Jairus, or the brother of Mary, did so with the ease of one who is stooping to do something that is quite within his power. The woman of Zarephath said to Elijah, when she received her son, " Now I know that thou art a man of God;" but when Jesus came forth, in the royalty of His own might, from the tomb of Joseph, He was powerfully "declared to be the Son of God." Elijah was great, but Jesus was pre-eminently greater; and when, upon the Mount of Transfiguration, the voice from the excellent glory made proclamation, "This is My beloved son, in whom I am well pleased: hear ye Him,"

Elijah himself was forward to do Jesus homage.
While, therefore, we do honour to the servant, let us
not forget to do still greater honour to the Lord.
Elijah is a man of God ; Jesus is the God of man,
yea, the God-man, the Alpha and the Omega, the
First and the Last, who alone can say, " I am He
that liveth, and was dead ; and behold, I am alive
for evermore, Amen ; and have the keys of hell and
of death."

But now, leaving the miracle to speak for itself, let
us group under a few observations the practical lessons
from this whole subject.

Let us learn, in the first place, that no circumstances insure exemption from disturbing unsettlements in God's providence. The members of this
household in Zarephath might without any presumption have supposed that they were, for the time,
under the special protection of Jehovah. Elijah had
been sent thither by the express command of God,
with the promise that he should be sustained. His
support had come to him through the kindness of a
widow, who had been rewarded for her benevolence
by God's continued and miraculous provision, and it
was still essential that he should be for some time
longer an inmate of her dwelling. Hence, if one
may ever be warranted to believe that all evil will be
warded off from himself and those connected with
him, surely Elijah might have so believed in the case
before us. But, lo ! even at such a time we have an
illustration of the great law that God's people are
ever liable to providential disturbances and dislodg-
ments, for just then the child of this widow suddenly
expired. Now, if we have such a thing as trial coming

here in such uncommon circumstances, how much more may we expect it in our ordinary lives? We talk of being comfortably settled! Alas! we know not what we say. We might as well speak of a ship as settled in mid-ocean. Ever as we think that, like Elijah here, we have got into some quiet resting-place, there comes some unlooked-for trouble, that puts our faith to the proof, and dissipates all our fondest imaginations of permanency. When we are beginning to feel comfortable, and saying to ourselves, now we shall have a breathing-time, some singular combination of circumstances, the possibility of which we had not foreseen or even conceived of, comes and deranges all our plans, as it says to us, "Ye have tarried long enough in this arbour of ease : arise, and go forward ; for through much tribulation you must enter the kingdom."

Thus we are sent through the experience which the Psalmist describes in these familiar words : "In my prosperity I said, I shall never be moved ; Lord, by Thy favour thou hast made my mountain to stand strong : thou didst hide Thy face, and I was troubled." We are never exempt from trouble. Yea, even in circumstances when it might almost seem that we could calculate on continuing as we are, it is sometimes the case that our sorest trials come upon us. Herein is that saying true, "It is the unexpected that happens ;" and never, so long as we are upon the earth, dare we count upon immunity from calamity. Neither character, nor privilege, nor the commission of God to do some great work in His service, will insure us against tribulation. Something will evermore come to shake us out of our security, and to make us feel that we know not what a day may bring forth. We may have deliverance from some great evil which for long we have been anticipating, even as this woman and her son were saved from death by famine; but in some new form, and in some unlooked-for manner, affliction will come upon us "to humble us, and to prove us, and to know what is in our hearts, whether we will serve the Lord or no." Thus we are kept ever on the watch to teach us entire dependence upon God Himself. He is the unchangeable rock; they who build on Him shall never be moved. But if we seek to raise our Babel tower of permanent happiness on any earthly foundation, we shall soon be put to confusion. It were as wise to found a house on the seamy side of Vesuvius, with the constant danger of being shaken by the upheavings of the mountain, or buried beneath the fiery lava and the burning ashes, as to attempt to build abiding felicity on an earthly thing, or to hope for undisturbed settlement in this fleeting world. "They build too low who build beneath the skies."

Let us learn, in the second place, that these providential unsettlements reveal us to ourselves, by placing us face to face with God. When this child died, his mother cried to the prophet, "Art thou come to bring my sin to remembrance, and to slay my son?" Clearly, therefore, there was some sin-stain upon her conscience; and though we dare not say that the iniquity caused the death of her child, yet God, through that dispensation, opened her eyes to her guilt and danger. All through her experience of famine, with death daily coming nearer, her conscience, so far as appears, was asleep; nor was it roused to action by her experience of God's goodness in sending her deliverance through the visit of Elijah.

But now there comes upon her a new trial, severe in the proportion in which it was unexpected, and she cries, " I am a sinner."

Nor is this any singular experience. It is by such sudden and unsettling providences yet that God reveals us to ourselves. The strain of the storm makes manifest the weak point in the vessel, and stirs up the mariner to have it strengthened. So the tension of trial shows where the character is defective ; and if we wisely learn the lesson, we will seek at once to have it renewed. How often has the careless sinner been aroused, first to agony and then to conversion, by the coming on him of some unlooked-for calamity ! Had things continued to go smoothly and prosperously with him, his conscience would have slumbered on, and no salvation would have been sought by him ; but trouble has revealed need, and need has impelled to prayer ; and the answer to the prayer has been the new and higher life of the soul.

Thus unbroken prosperity is not by any means a blessing to the sinner. The Psalmist has put this thought most suggestively when he says of some, " Because they have no changes, therefore, they fear not God ;" and, in the same connection we all remember that Jeremiah says of Moab, " He hath been at ease from his youth, and he hath settled on his lees, and hath not been emptied from vessel to vessel, neither hath he gone into captivity : therefore his taste remained in him, and his scent is not changed." An English poet has said that " we rise on stepping-stones of our dead selves to higher things ;" but only by calamity such as that which came upon this woman are our evil selves revealed

and slain; that is, if we learn its lesson rightly.
Therefore, to those who improve it properly, beneath
the rough and outer rind of the trial there is a kernel
of sweet and wholesome nutriment.

But remember: to have the blessing, we must
renounce the evil which the calamity reveals, and
turn from it unto the Lord. How has it been with
you, my brethren, when these unsettlements have
come upon you? Have you been benefited by
them? Have they drained off from you the lees of
iniquity in which you had been settling? Happy
they who have been shaken out of themselves, no
matter at what cost, if only they have found the
Lord! But if we have refused to learn from God's
dislodging dealings with us, we may expect yet
heavier sorrows; and if these be disregarded, then,
heaviest of all, we may prepare for everlasting doom.
You know how you shuddered before God as He
came to you in your earthly trial; but if that were so,
how will you stand aghast as you meet Him before
His awful throne of judgment! In mercy God has
sent these minor trials before the last and severest of
all, that from the knowledge of ourselves which they
have given us we may be stirred up to prepare for
that which is still before us. But if we could not
endure the lighter, how shall we bear the heavier?
"If thou hast run with the footmen, and they have
wearied thee, then how canst thou contend with
horses? and if in the land of peace, wherein thou
trustedst, they wearied thee, then how wilt thou do
in the swelling of Jordan?"[1]

---

[1] Jeremiah xii. 5.

Notice, thirdly, that these unsettling providences only furnish the believer with a new errand to God's throne of grace. Behold how calm Elijah was all through this trying season! He felt the child's death keenly : deeply, too, he felt the mother's recrimination ; yet he is not shaken out of his faith by the shock. Nay, rather his confidence in God is only stimulated to new boldness, as he carries the body up to his chamber, and beseeches God that the soul may come into it again. Our affliction is sanctified to us when it sends us more earnestly to our knees. Had Elijah been moved to say, "To what purpose is all my earnestness in Jehovah's service, if those who befriend me are to be thus distressed?" or had he determined that he would abjure his allegiance to Jehovah, then he would have shown that his zeal had not been rightly rooted or deeply cherished. But when, in the hour of his perplexity, he goes straight to God, we have a new proof of the genuineness of his piety. Tell me where a man goes first in the hour of sorrow and unsettlement, and I will tell you his character. You cannot hesitate about Hezekiah's piety, when you see him spread Rabshakeh's letter before the Lord ; you can have no doubt about that of Nehemiah, when you read of his praying to God while yet his master's cup was in his hand ; nor can you have any uncertainty about that of Paul, when you observe that his thorn in the flesh sent him to his Lord. Whither did you go in trouble? On whom did you call for deliverance? To whom did you cling for support? Answer these questions honestly, and you will know whether or not you are the children of God ; and if haply you find that you are not yet

numbered among his sons, give no sleep to your eyes
until you have secured the priceless blessing of adoption through faith in Him who died for our sins,
according to the Scriptures.

Finally, observe that the deliverance which God
gives to His people in the time of their unsettlement,
and in answer to their prayers, leads them to a more
assured confidence in Himself. This woman had a
firmer faith in Elijah than ever after she had received
her son alive at his hands; but Elijah himself had
more confidence than ever in his God. Indeed, if
we will consider it rightly, we shall see that it was by
such experiences as this that Jehovah was training
His servant up to that sublimity of faith and courage
which he evinced on Mount Carmel, when he confronted Ahab and the priests and prophets of Baal.
You perhaps at first are disposed to marvel at the
boldness of the proposals which he made that day.
I confess I have often done so; but now, when I
think of his bearing on that memorable occasion, in
its connection with the antecedent incidents in his
history, my wonder disappears. Elijah would not
have dared to make such proposals to Ahab, or to
offer such prayers to Jehovah as he then did, had it
not been for the fact that God had heard and
answered prayers of similar boldness which he had
already presented. It was easy for him to ask fire to
come down and consume his sacrifice, after he had
seen God restore a dead child to life in response to
his entreaty. Take his procedure on Carmel by
itself, apart from all the other chapters in his life, and
it does seem marvellously strange; but look at it as
the last and highest of a series of experiences of the

power of prayer, and it seems perfectly natural. By
the triumphs of his former faith he had ascended to
that confidence which he manifested on the great
occasion which proved to be the highest tide-mark of
his career.

But it has been so with all the great ones in the
peerage of faith. Look at Abraham; and as you see
him ascending Moriah to sacrifice his son, you wonder
at the calm sublimity of his heroic obedience. You
think it almost superhuman. You cannot understand how he attained to it. But when you go back
over his previous history, the whole thing is explained.
He could not have reached this altitude by one
bounding leap, but by all those unsettlements and
trials which came upon him from the day when he
left the far land of Ur; and by the grace which
brought him through them all, God had led him up,
step by step, to this last and terrible ordeal, which
was also his crowning triumph. His experience, oft
repeated, and each time with added elements of
grace, of God's faithfulness on occasions of necessity,
enabled him to overcome in that supreme moment
of uttermost extremity. So, again, with Paul. Look
at his calmness as, confronting death, he said, "I am
now ready to be offered," and you will find that it is
the natural result of the experiences of his life. In
his many perils Jesus had been beside him. Amidst
the dangers that beset him in Corinth; in the prison
at Jerusalem; on the deck of the drifting ship, ere
yet it went to pieces on the Maltese shore; before
magistrates and judges and imperial governors, Christ
had been his faithful friend, and had fulfilled to him
His word of promise. Therefore he could trust Him

thoroughly once more, and say, "I know whom I have believed."

Thus, while unsettlements reveal the soul to itself, they also reveal the Saviour to the soul; and he who has been supported through them by His grace in the past can look forward with calm assurance to the future, feeling that everything will be well. The God who, in answer to prayer, did not refuse to restore the child to life, would not, Elijah was sure, leave him dishonoured before Baal's priests on Carmel; and He who has been with us in the checkered scenes of life will not forsake us when we come to die. Each new deliverance He gives us is a new stimulus to faith; and the more numerous such experiences are, the more heroic does our faith become. The result is glorious, though some stages of the process may be bitter. This "now I know" of the woman, in its clear assurance, was worth the agony of the trial through which she attained it; and while we are feeling the heaviness of calamity, we may solace ourselves with the thought that our experience under it will remain with us, for stimulus and support, through every after-affliction. Thus the riddle of Manoah's son repeats itself. In the carcass of the slain lion there is a precious honey-comb. "Out of the eater comes forth meat, and out of the bitter comes forth sweetness."

V.

RE-APPEARANCE.

1 KINGS xviii. 1–19.

THE opening verse in this chapter contains two
marks of time—the one indefinite, in the phrase
"after many days;" the other somewhat precise, in
the clause "in the third year." The former of these
refers, in my judgment, to the duration of Elijah's
sojourn at Zarephath; the latter to that of the
drought throughout the land. This view of the case,
indeed, involves a slight appearance of discrepancy
between the statement here made and that which is
repeated twice in the New Testament, as to the time
during which the famine lasted; for it will be remembered that both our Lord Jesus Himself and the
apostle James have spoken of the drought in Elijah's
days as having continued for "three years and six
months."[1] Some have attempted to remove this
difficulty by alleging that the words translated "in
the third year" might with equal propriety be
rendered "after the third year;" but as I have not
been able to verify this assertion by any incontrovertible instance, I prefer the explanation given by Dr.
Jamieson, which is to the following effect: "The

[1] Luke iv. 25; James v. 17.

early rain in Palestine fell in our March, the latter
rain in our October. Though Ahab might at first
have ridiculed Elijah's announcement, yet when
neither of these rains fell in its season, he was
incensed against the prophet as the cause of the
nation's suffering, and compelled him to consult his
safety by concealment. Now, this might have been six
months after the king had been told that there should
be neither dew nor rain; and from this period the
three years in this passage may be computed, whereas
the three years and six months of the New Testament
may be reckoned from the date when Elijah first
confronted Ahab."[1] In any case, toward the end of
three years and six months after his former visit to
the king, "the word of the Lord came to the prophet
at Zarephath saying, Go, show thyself unto Ahab, and
I will send rain upon the earth."

With mingled feelings of sadness and of delight,
we may be sure that Elijah received this command.
It enjoined him to leave a home where, for at least
two years, he had been retired and happy, and to bid
farewell to his Gentile hostess and her boy, both of
whom had become objects of special interest to him,
and he could not part from them without regret.
But, on the other hand, if I have read his character
correctly, he delighted in activity, more especially
when there was added to it the exciting element of
danger. Hence, as the eager warrior hastens to the
battle-field, Elijah was positively attracted to the conflict that was before him, the rather as he recognised

---

[1] "Commentary, Critical, Experimental, and Practical, on the
Old and New Testaments," by Jamieson, Fausset, and Brown,
vol. ii. p. 352.

in it the opportunity of his life, when, as the servant
of Jehovah, he should be able to strike a decisive
blow at the Baalism of the court and the indifferent-
ism of the country. On the whole, therefore, while
sorry to leave his hostess and her boy, we may believe
that he was rather glad than otherwise to be recalled
to public service, and that he took his way toward
Samaria, not only without dismay, but with the
earnestness of a man who felt himself " straightened,"
until his perilous work was accomplished.

But, alas ! what a dismal prospect met his gaze at
every step of his journey ! In very deed, " the
famine was sore in the land." No waving corn-fields
or leafy vineyards could he anywhere perceive ! Not
even a patch of green appeared to rest his eye with
its refreshing verdure ! Nor was there near any
dwelling the barn-yard, with its store of plenty, as of
yore. All was brown and barren desolation. No
sounds of joy fell upon his ear. The harp of nature
was for the time unstrung. The purling of brooks,
the carol of birds, the lowing of cattle were heard no
more. The song of the reaper, the mirth of the
vintage, and the joy of harvest-home were things for
the time unknown ; for " the Lord had caused to
cease from the cities of Israel and from the streets
of Samaria the voice of mirth and the voice of gladness, the voice of the bridegroom and the voice of
the bride, for the land had become desolate." Again,
as at the first, " the ground was cursed for man's
sake," and men were taught anew that it is an evil
thing and a bitter to forsake the Lord.

As the prophet went on toward the city of Ahab's
residence, he met a cavalcade under the leadership
of the king's steward, going forth to survey a wide

tract of country, to see whether any fountain of water could be discovered, or any patches of grass, so that, if possible, the royal horses and mules might be preserved alive. Such an excursion is an indication of the terrible extent to which the famine had gone, especially when we take in connection with it the fact that Ahab himself had gone forth with another party on a similar errand, but in a different direction. It seems strange, indeed, to us that a king and his steward should have gone personally on such missions ; but this is only one among many illustrations that might be given of the primitive manners of Eastern magnates. Even at this day something of the same sort may be seen among the emirs of Arabia, and the chiefs of Central Asia, for, according to Dr. Kitto, " none of these high personages would think it in any way beneath their dignity to lead an expedition in search of grass or water. The matter is, indeed, regarded as of so much importance that it is a sort of official duty in them to conduct the search ; and success in it contributes very materially to their popularity among their people, who are apt to ascribe the happy result in a great measure, if not wholly, to the fortune of their chief." [1]

It is another instance of the special providence of God, that the steward Obadiah, with whom Elijah was now brought into contact, was a sincere adherent to Jehovah. He was not at all such a person as one would have expected to find in a post of honour in Ahab's house. From his youth up he had been a devout servant of the Lord. He had not seen his

[1] " Daily Bible Illustrations," vol. iv. p. 252.

way, indeed, to follow the example of those priests
and Levites and servants of Jehovah who, in the days
of Jeroboam, left their lands behind them, and went
into the country of Judah, in order that they might
enjoy the privilege of worshipping the God of Israel
according to the Mosaic ritual.[1]   But, still, he was a
true servant of the Lord.   Perhaps Ahab overlooked
his piety, because he valued his character as a servant,
and could ill afford to do without him.   Probably,
also, Jezebel was deterred from urging his dismissal
or his death, because she knew how indispensable to
his comfort Ahab believed Obadiah to be.   But, however it came about, he was the steward of Ahab's
house.   Yet, though he held that position, he was
true to Jehovah, and his very presence in the palace
enabled him to do signal service to some of his
brethren.   For when Jezebel had endeavoured to
destroy all the schools of the prophets in the land,
and had put to death most of the young men who
were students at these institutions, Obadiah was the
means of sheltering and feeding no fewer than one
hundred, whom he had concealed " by fifties in a
cave."   Thus, though this good man had not himself
the martyr spirit of Elijah, he had the heart to help
God's servants ; and he used the position which he
held in such a way as to protect those who were in
danger.   He had faith, but he had not added to it
the highest degree of courage.   He had some courage,
indeed ; for without that he would not have dared to
shelter the prophets, and feed them in the cave ; but
he had not such a kind and measure of courage as to

_____

[1] 2 Chronicles xi. 13-17.

stand openly out and avow himself the protector of
his brethren, and one with them in faith. Or,
perhaps, we may explain his conduct in another way.
It is possible that he felt he could really do more to
help forward the Lord's cause where he was than he
could elsewhere, and so he kept his post in Ahab's
house. At any rate, there he was, like "a lily among
thorns;" and one cannot but observe the providence
which brought him and Elijah together before the
prophet went to meet the king.

As soon as Obadiah saw him, he recognised him,
and said, "Art thou that my lord Elijah?" where-
upon he answered, "1 am : go, tell thy lord, Behold,
Elijah is here." This order greatly disconcerted the
timid Obadiah. He knew that Ahab had hatred
enough for Elijah to put him to death; but he
believed also that God loved His servant too well to
allow him to fall a victim to the royal violence.
Hence he feared that if he went to give Elijah's
message to the monarch, God would in some way or
other take the prophet away; and then the king,
foiled in his anticipated revenge, would turn upon
him with the fury of a wild beast that has been
robbed of its prey. He was, therefore, most unwilling
to do as Elijah had commanded, and he regarded
the fact that he should be asked to do anything of
the kind as an indication that he had committed
some special sin for which some signal punishment
was to come upon him. Naturally, therefore, he
rehearsed to the prophet, not in the way of vainglory,
but as an indication of his true-hearted sincerity, how
he had preserved from the intolerance of Jezebel no
fewer than a hundred of the sons of the prophets.

His touching appeal elicited from Elijah a most solemn asseveration that he would really confront Ahab ; and, so fortified, Obadiah went and told his master, who speedily came to meet the prophet.

As he drew near, determined to have whatever of advantage the first word might afford, the king, with much swagger and show of indignation, said, "Art. thou he that troubleth Israel?" He had no word to say of his own sin ; he forgot the iniquity of the people of the land, of which he had been the insti-gator, and in which he had been the leader; he took no note of the hand of Jehovah in the calamity which had come upon his kingdom, and spoke as if the whole matter had been a mere personal difference between him and Elijah. He traced the drought only to the prophet. He cast the entire blame of it upon him. Much as if one suffering under a painful disease should blame the doctor for producing it, because, knowing the habits of the patient, he had predicted that it would come. But Elijah was not the man to be browbeaten into silence by the words of an angry monarch ; and so, with no mere vulgar recrimination, but with the calm dignity of the faithful preacher who desired to send the arrow quivering into his hearer's heart, he made reply, "I have not troubled Israel; but thou, and thy father's house, in that ye have forsaken the commandments of the Lord, and thou hast followed Baalim." And then he pro-posed that a solemn assembly of the people should be convened on Mount Carmel, when, in the pre-sence of Israel's thousands, the controversy between Jehovah and Baal might be settled by Elijah as the representative of the one, and the four hundred and fifty prophets of Baal as the partisans of the other. To such a proposal the king could make no plausible objection. So they parted to prepare for the dread encounter, Elijah in the solitude of communion with God, Ahab in the palace of Jezreel, surrounded by Jezebel and her favourite priests.

There let us leave them for the time, while we dwell a while on some practical reflections which are suggested by the history which we have now rehearsed. We have here three characters: first, a godly man, Obadiah; second, an ungodly man, Ahab; and, third, the servant of the Lord, Elijah, dealing with each of the others according to his character.

Let us look, first, at the godly man. As I have already hinted, he is found where we should scarcely have thought of seeking for him. He is in the service, yea, in the very house, of the idolatrous Ahab. Yet even there he is seeking conscientiously to do God's work. Now, this is by no means an unusual thing. Commonly we think of the army as a profession in which religion is at a discount; and when one hears of a youth enlisting, he is apt to fear that he is going all astray. Yet Cornelius was an officer in a Roman legion, and some of Paul's most interesting converts belonged to the barracks of the Imperial City. So, in more modern times, the names of Cromwell, Gustavus Adolphus, Gardiner, Havelock, Vicars, Howard, and a host of others, will immediately occur to us as illustrations of the fact that most devoted Christians may be found among military men. Similarly, there are certain localities into which one would scarcely go with the expectation of discovering an ardent follower of Jesus. There are

streets in all large cities which have such an evil
reputation that you would no more think of entering
them to look for a Christian than you would of going
to seek for a tropical plant within the arctic circle.
Yet every district visitor will corroborate me when I
say that sometimes, even in these uninviting neigh-
bourhoods, you will come upon such specimens of
faith, of integrity, of cheerfulness, and of purity, as
will gladden your heart, and encourage you in the
work you are attempting to perform.   If the question,
" Can there any good thing come out of Nazareth ? "
had been permitted to weigh with him exclusively,
Nathanael had not recognised even the Lord Jesus
Christ.   So we must beware of coming to a hasty
judgment of a man's character from the simple consideration of the place in which we have found him,
and of the circumstances by which he is surrounaed.

But there is another department in which we may
apply this lesson.   It is most instructive to us in its
bearing on ecclesiastical matters.   We must distinguish, for example, between the Roman Catholic
Church, as such, and many of those who may be
found, so to say, in its house.   It would be unjust as
well as uncharitable in us to suppose that, at the era
of the Reformation, Luther had no friends or
sympathisers, who yet for reasons, which to themselves, at least, were sufficient, never left the Church
in which they had been reared.   We honour, indeed,
in the highest degree the great Reformer as a second
Elijah ; but we must not forget that Christ had even
then many Obadiahs who remained within the Church
of Rome.   Just as in this old history, this royal
steward had neither gone to Judah, like the priests

and Levites who had left their lands in Jeroboam's day, nor had publicly identified himself with Elijah, while yet he was a sincere friend of God's servants, and a devout worshipper of the Lord himself; so I can imagine a guileless, timid soul remaining, even in the excitement of controversy, within the Roman Catholic Church, under the idea that he could do more for Christ and for His servants there than he could do elsewhere. Of course, we all see that if every believer in the doctrine of justification by faith alone had acted on this principle, there would have been no Reformation; and we instinctively feel that the prudence or policy of those who did so act had overshadowed their courage. Yet we may—nay, must—admit that they were sincere followers of God up to the measure of their light; nor can we forget that at different eras there have been men in that Church like Bernard, and Lyra, and Fénélon, and Pascal.

I might easily illustrate the same principle by other historic cases. Thus, it would be wrong to declare that all the good and faithful ministers left the Church of England on that black Bartholomew-day when the two thousand Nonconformists left their parishes, their pulpits, and their parsonages for Christ. So again, in Scotland, we cannot help sympathising, both politically and ecclesiastically, with the noble stand made by the Covenanters—a stand which did more than many things to win civil and religious freedom for Great Britain; but neither, on the other hand, can we unqualifiedly condemn the good Leighton, who was induced to accept a bishopric under the idea that in such a position he might do something to heal the divisions of his native country. No one can read his Commentary on First Peter without discovering that its author was a heavenly-minded man ; and though he was in the house of Ahab when he was Bishop of Dunkeld, still he was a godly man there, and is not to be ostracised without mercy for his mitre's sake. Again, in more recent times, it is within the knowledge of the present generation that the controversy which resulted in the formation of the Free Church of Scotland was mainly carried on between those who were decidedly evangelical, and those who were cold Moderates, who dealt in moral essays, and passed the Gospel " by on the other side ;" yet it would be absurd to maintain that all the good people and all the evangelical ministers left the Scotch Church at the Disruption. We must distinguish between the character of the man and the place in which we find him. He may be in what we consider a house of Ahab, but he may be an Obadiah still.

But passing from this aspect of the subject, let us go a step further, and say that the godly man may serve Jehovah in almost any circumstances. Obadiah managed to keep a good conscience, even in Ahab's house, and he used his position to render a kind of service to Jehovah's cause which even Elijah himself could not have given. I do not suppose that there was another man at that time in the country who could, without suspicion and with thorough security, have protected the prophets of the Lord save himself, and he did it admirably. He might have made his office an excuse for doing nothing ; but, instead, he made it the means of accomplishing a great deal.

And in other things he acted conscientiously. He never bowed the knee to Baal; and he kept himself clear of the national apostasy. No doubt this might cost him the favour of Jezebel; but that he did not regard. He rendered unto Ahab the things which were Ahab's, and unto God the things which were God's. Now, this may teach us that we should never allow our circumstances to keep us from doing what we believe to be right. Nehemiah could serve God in a Persian palace; Daniel and his three friends could retain their integrity in a Babylonian college; and Paul could turn the tent-maker's shop, wherein he laboured at Corinth, into a school for Christ.

You often hear it said, as an excuse for one's lack of earnestness in the Christian life, or for his falling into positive sin, " You must remember the exposed position in which he is placed, and make allowance for his circumstances." The artisans whose daily craft takes them into the roughest places of the city are apt to say, "Just think of the temptations that confront us everywhere all along these rivers, and of the sort of people we are continually meeting." The sailor will exclaim, "How do you suppose we can maintain a Christian character on shipboard? You don't know what a swearing lot surrounds us, or if you did, you would understand at once that it's use-less trying to be religious at sea." Nor are these the only classes who would thus apologise for their con-formity to the world. In our counting-rooms and workshops, and on the floors of our exchanges, there are not a few who say, in effect, words like these: " Religion is all very well for the fireside and for the church, but we cannot be regulated by its maxims in business;" and who give us to understand that if they were to act in their daily callings on the principles of the Sermon on the Mount, they would soon find themselves in the Bankruptcy Court. But is it so? Is it, indeed, the case that men cannot serve God in the workshop, and in the ship, and in the store? So much the worse, if it be so, for these occupations ; for if we cannot honour God in them, then they must be in and of themselves sinful, and must be given up. But is it so? Have there been no eminent Christians among our successful merchants, or our skilled operatives, or our noble seamen? There have ; and I fearlessly assert that if our business or trade be not sinful, as playing on the credulity of men, or ministering to their vices, we may serve God in it, whatever it be, or whithersoever it takes us. Nay, the more difficulties we have to contend against, the greater ultimately will be our strength of character. Timid as he was, Obadiah was a more courageous man in Ahab's house than he would have been elsewhere, for the resistance which he there met with developed strength in him. Like the palm-tree, the Christian character grows firmer by being weighted, and becomes hardier by being exposed to opposition.

I have somewhere read the following incident in the life of a distinguished botanist. Being exiled from his native land, he obtained employment as an under-gardener in the service of a nobleman. While he was in this situation, his master received a valuable plant, the nature and habits of which were unknown to him. It was given to the gardener to be taken care of, and he, fancying it to be a tropical production, put it into the hot-house (for it was winter), and dealt with it as with the others under the glass. But it began to decay. He brought his master to look at it. They thought it dying, and, as a last resort, they were going to put it in a yet hotter chamber, when the strange under-gardener asked permission to examine it. As soon as he looked at it he said, "This is an arctic plant: you are killing it by the tropical heat into which you have introduced it." So he took it outside, and exposed it to the frost, and, to the dismay of the upper-gardener, heaped pieces of ice around the flower-pot; but the result vindicated his wisdom, for straightway it began to recover, and was soon as strong as ever. Now, such a plant is Christian character. It is not difficulty that is dangerous to it, but ease. Put it into a hot-house, separate it from the world, surround it with luxury, hedge it in from every opposition, and you take the surest means of killing it. But take it out into the frost, let it meet and overcome temptation in the way of daily duty, let it come into contact, as it seeks to do its work, with the icy spirit of the world ; in a word, let it have to contend with difficulty, and you thereby nurture it into strength. Do not I speak truth in all this? Where will you find nobler, manlier, or more admirable specimens of Christianity than among our merchants, our seamen, and our artisans? When they are truly Christ's, they are also nobly and magnificently His. Tell me not, therefore, that you cannot serve God where you are. You know better. You know you can, if you will. Be it that you are in the house of Ahab; then you may yet be like Obadiah there, and keep yourself unspotted from its idolatry.

But now we turn to the contemplation of the ungodly man, Ahab; and the first thing we see about him in this affair is the utter selfishness by which he was actuated. He went himself in one direction, and sent Obadiah in another, to scour the country for supplies; but for what? that he might feed the famishing multitudes of Israel? No; but that he might save his horses and mules alive! Thus the animals that contributed to his dignity, or ministered to his ease, were of more importance to him than the lives of his subjects. Heartless man! you say; and yet how much of the same sort of thing there is even in this so-called Christian land! What extremes of luxury and misery meet and touch each other in this city! Within the home of affluence, you will see, beneath the lustre of many lamps, the throng of beauty and fashion, attired in dresses of the richest fabric and the fairest hue. They enjoy themselves to the uttermost with music and dance, and then adjourn to the feast of plenty; while outside, in the chill darkness, within hearing of the mirth that falls like hailstones on her heart, sits on a door-step a poor child of shame, shivering in the frost, and pining with hunger! Alas! alas! is it not true of too many among us that they pet their horses, and pamper their lap-dogs, while they forget the misery of their fellow-men? With what scathing scorn has Miss Procter exposed this sore evil in her native land! and, as to some extent it is true also of

ourselves, I may be pardoned for introducing her
lines here :—

" It is cold, dark midnight ; yet listen
　　To the patter of tiny feet.
　Is it one of your dogs, fair lady,
　　Who whines in the bleak cold street ?
　Is it one of your silken spaniels
　　Shut out in the snow and sleet ? "

" My dogs sleep warm in their baskets,
　　Safe from the darkness and snow ;
　All the beasts in our Christian England
　　Find pity wherever they go.
　Those are only the homeless children
　　Who are wandering to and fro."

" Look out in the gusty darkness—
　　I have seen it again and again,
　That shadow that flits so slowly
　　Up and down, past the window-pane.
　It is surely some criminal lurking
　　Out there in the frozen rain ? "

" Nay, our criminals all are sheltered,
　　They are pitied and taught and fed :
　That is only a sister-woman,
　　Who has got neither food nor bed.
　And the Night cries, ' Sin to be living ; '
　　And the River cries, ' Sin to be dead ! ' "

" Look out at that farthest corner,
　　Where the walls stand blank and bare :
　Can that be a pack which a peddler
　　Has left and forgotten there ;
　His goods lying out, unsheltered,
　　Will be spoilt by the damp night air."

" Nay, goods in our thrifty England
　　Are not left to lie and grow rotten ;

For each man knows the value
Of silk or woollen or cotton,
But in counting the riches of England,
I think our poor are forgotten.

" Our beasts and our thieves and our chattels
Have weight for good or for ill;
But the poor are only *His* image,
His presence, *His* word, *His* will :
And so Lazarus lies at our door-step,
And Dives neglects him still." [1]

" But what would you have?" you say ; "must we
have nothing that we can do without, while others
are starving? Must we literally sell all that we have,
and give to the poor?" To which I answer, "That
certainly is not required of every one ; and in.
matters of this sort it is not possible for any man to
draw a hard and fast line. These things must be
left to the conscience of each ; only let us seek to
have our consciences enlightened by God's Word and
Spirit regarding them.

In general, however, this principle holds good, that
we must not indulge ourselves in luxuries to the
neglect of the claims of God's cause or God's poor
upon us. It is only after we have discharged our
consciences of all obligations under which we lie to
the poor, and to the cause of Christ, that we are
warranted to turn to our horses and our carriages
and our luxuries. Have you done your duty to the
poor? Have you met the cries of distress that are
rising on your ear? Have you given as God has
prospered you to the cause of home and foreign

[1] "A Chaplet of Verses," by Adelaide A. Procter.

missions, with which the glory of the Lord is so inseparably connected? Have you done as much as in you lay to lift that load of debt from a noble institution that is doing daily service in the Master's cause? Then enjoy your luxuries, take the benefit of your carriage, and have, at the same time, the satisfaction that you are sharing your happiness with many others.

Furthermore, I think this is also a safe and wholesome rule : that with every increase in our expenditure upon ourselves, whether in house, or in dress, or in thanksgiving festivities, we should make a corresponding increase in our donations to the cause of God and of the needy. We ought to feel it to be a mockery of Jehovah to load ourselves with ornaments, and surround ourselves with luxuries, while, when we are asked to give to His cause or to His people, we say, " We cannot afford it." Cannot afford it ! Then sacrifice some glittering jewel, or some mantel-piece ornament, or give a party less in the season, rather than make that humiliating confession. We are the stewards of God's bounty ; and what will He say to us at last, when we declare that we spent so much upon ourselves that we had nothing left to spend on Him? Go, my brethren ; be warned by the selfishness of Ahab here, and take example rather from the poor widow of the former chapter, who, though at the brink of starvation, and about to prepare her last meal, gave the first portion to a fellow-sufferer, and received in return a blessing from the Lord.

But, we must remark also, regarding Ahab's conduct here, that the consequence of ungodliness is blindness. See how he comes up to Elijah with the greatest confidence, as if no blame could be thrown upon himself, and the whole calamity were due to the prophet, " Art thou he that troubleth Israel?" His conscience had become blunted by continual transgression, so that it ceased to record the evil which he had committed, or to upbraid him for it. There is a point at which the mercury in the thermometer is itself frozen, and marks no lower degree of cold ; and there is a point in the sinner's career when his moral sense becomes torpid, and takes no further note of guilt. Ahab had, I fear, reached that stage in reference to his idolatry, and so he charged Elijah with causing that which was the result of his own sin.

My hearer, unconverted ! will you take warning from this case ? If you persist in your course, your heart will be hardened into impenetrability; you will become "past feeling," and will meet every messenger of God as if he were a guilty troubler of the community, while you are irreproachable. Thus does the moral nature become positively perverted, putting light for darkness and darkness for light, sweet for bitter and bitter for sweet, good for evil and evil for good. Oh, beware of sinning yourself into such a state ! Get a good conscience through faith in Jesus Christ; and keep a good conscience by obedience unto Him. Let the eye be single, that your whole body may be full of light ; for, " if the light that is in thee be darkness, how great is that darkness ! "

I have now time only for the merest glance at the manner in which the servant of God dealt with each of these men, according to his character. With

Obadiah, the prophet was considerate and tender, seeking even by an oath to remove all cause of anxiety from his heart. With Ahab, he was stern and unbending, so that soon he who came with a swagger went away with a halt. Thus, the true minister of Christ will seek to have words in season for each, according to the disposition of those with whom he comes into contact. With some he will be "gentle as a nurse, cherishing her children;" others he will rebuke sharply. With some he will expostulate tearfully; others he will take by the hand and lead lovingly forward. What a perfect example in this, as in all other respects, has our Lord Jesus left us! He spake in one strain to the sincere but timid Nicodemus, in another to the hypocritical scribes and Pharisees. He dealt in one way with the woman at the well, and in another with the trembling one who came behind Him, seeking almost to steal a cure. He loved the young man who came to Him inquiring the way, but retired sorrowfully, not yet prepared to part with his possessions; but He replied with sternness to those who sought to entangle Him in His talk.

Brethren, "he that winneth souls is wise." Oh, may God give us who are in the ministry grace and wisdom to say the right thing to the right person at the right time! When one is thus wise as a preacher, he finds "acceptable words, even words of truth,' and as he utters them, they become like "goads, or as nails fastened by the masters of assemblies." Seek not to deal with every one after some unvarying method. As the physician suits his prescription to the disease, so let the Christian worker adapt his method to the character of him with whom he has to deal. It is right sometimes to be gentle, and it is right sometimes to be stern; but wisdom is needed to know when each is better. Had Jesus spoken to Nicodemus as He did to those who devoured widows' houses, and for a pretence made long prayers, we should never have heard of the ruler of the Jews again. Let him who would be useful, therefore, study human nature as well as the Gospel of the Lord, that he may know " to give to each his portion of meat in due season." But when sternness and severity are required, let us be sure that underneath there is a heart full of love to our fellow-sinner and of loyalty to the Lord whom we serve. The sternest things are then the strongest when the tear-drop quivers in the eyes of him who speaks them.

VI.

THE CONFLICT ON CARMEL.

1 KINGS xviii. 21.

ON the shores of the Levant, and immediately to
the south of Acre, there is a range of hills
stretching out for five or six miles, and terminating
in a somewhat rugged and precipitous promontory.
The highest peak, resembling a flattened cone in
shape, rises about fifteen hundred feet above the level
of the sea, and is that which in Scripture is more
particularly called Mount Carmel. It is described as
the finest and most beautiful mountain in Palestine.
Even yet, though the land is lying under a curse,
there are evident traces of its former fertility; and in
olden times it seems to have answered exactly to its
name, which signifies "a fruitful field," or "a country
of gardens and vineyards." At its base flows "that
ancient river, the river Kishon," and away to the
eastward stretches the magnificent plain of Esdraelon,
terminating in the glory of Tabor and the mountains
of Jordan, while in the far distance northward we
catch a glimpse of the snowy peaks of Lebanon.

Turning round and looking toward the west, we
see, far as the eye can reach, the blue waves of the
Mediterranean shimmering in the sunbeam ; to the

right lies Acre, far beneath us; and to the left we take in the ruins of Cæsarea, the city on which Herod lavished his magnificence, and in which Paul delivered those unrivalled defences before Felix, Festus, and Agrippa.

Wherever we look there is either some beauty to satisfy the eye, or some historical association to stir the heart. Every name we mention brings up a memory with it, and he has no true soul within him who can look on such a landscape, in the light of history, without having his spirit roused into enthusiasm, or kindled into rapture.

On that plain before us, what battles have been fought! What questions, with the fate of nations trembling in the balance, have been settled! There Barak and Deborah vanquished the haughty Sisera; there Gideon overcame the Midianites; there the Philistines encountered Saul on that melancholy day when he fled before them to Gilboa, and, to escape their swords, fell upon his own; there the banners of the Crusaders have fluttered in the breeze, and the eagles of Napoleon have been wetted by the evening dews. Here, too, where we stand, on the inner side of Mount Carmel, and near the eastern extremity of the range, in a noble, natural amphitheatre, there was decided, in the most signal and solemn manner, the great question between God and Baal. And, as we gaze upon the scene, we seem to see again the assembled throng of Israel, and to hear anew the voice of the valiant Elijah ringing out, clear and loud, as with the notes of a trumpet, these pointed words: "How long halt ye between two opinions? if the Lord be God, follow Him : but if Baal, then follow him."

The exact spot where the events narrated in this chapter occurred has been thoroughly identified, and preserves in its name, *El Muhrakah*, "the sacrifice," a memorial of the event. I cannot better describe it than in the words of Dr. Porter, in his article on Mount Carmel, in Alexander's " Kitto " :—

" At the eastern extremity of the ridge, where the wooded heights of Carmel sink down into the usual bleakness of the hills of Palestine, is a terrace of natural rock. It is encompassed by dense thickets of evergreens, and upon it are the remains of an old and massive square structure, built of large hewed stones. This is ' *El Muhrakah*,' and here, in all probability, stood Elijah's altar. The situation and environs answer in every particular to the various incidents in the narrative. A short distance from the terrace is a fountain, whence the water may have been brought which was poured round Elijah's sacrifice and altar. The terrace commands a noble view over the whole plain of Esdraelon from the banks of the Kishon, down at the bottom of the steep declivity, away to the distant hill of Gilboa, at whose base stood the royal city of Jezreel. To the eight hundred and fifty prophets ranged, doubtless, on the wide upland sweep just beneath the terrace ; to the multitudes of people, many of whom may have remained on the plain, the altar of Elijah would be in full view, and they could all see in the evening twilight that ' the fire of the Lord fell and consumed the burnt-offering, and the wood, and the stones, and the dust, and licked up the water.' The people, then trembling with fear and indignation, seized, at Elijah's bidding, the prophets of Baal, ' and Elijah brought them down to the brook Kishon, and slew them there.' On the lower declivities of the mountain is a mound called *Tell el-Kusis*, 'the hill of the priests,' which probably marks the very scene of the execution. May not the present name of the Kishon itself have originated in this tragic event, as it is called *Nahr-el-Mokatta*, 'the river of slaughter'? The prophet went up again to the altar, which is near, but not upon the summit of the mountain. While he prayed, he said to his servant, 'Go up, now, look toward the sea.' The sea is not visible from the terrace, but a few minutes' ascent leads to a peak which commands its whole expanse. And the modern name of the whole range of Carmel is *Jebel Mar Elias*, 'the mountain of St. Elijah.'"[1]

And now, having obtained a clear idea of the topography of the scene, let us endeavour to reproduce the events which were here enacted, and to gather up the lessons which they furnish for the present time.

When the summons went forth for the national gathering, the people anxiously speculated on the object for which the assembly was convened; and having learned to connect the name of Elijah with the terrible drought from which they had been suffering, they eagerly anticipated the appointed day. As it drew near, companies from every quarter of the land might be seen wending their way toward the spot; and, when the morning dawned, there stood upon the terrace and the plain a moving multitude of men such as has been seldom witnessed on the surface of the earth. Ere long, attended by the members of his court, the king appears, and passes on to the place

---

[1] Alexander's "Kitto": article *Carmel.*

of honour, marked by the spear fixed upright in the ground, which had been reserved for him. Again the crowd divides, and this time, with all the pomp and splendour of a stately procession, and arrayed in gorgeous vestments, the eight hundred and fifty priests and prophets of Baal march to their assigned position.

And now there is a pause. Men wonder if Elijah will indeed appear. Perhaps he has conveyed himself away; perhaps he has seen the pageant from a distance, and in despair has given up the contest. "What! think ye that he will not come?" is now the question; when, lo! across the shoulder of the mountain, fresh from communion with Jehovah, the man of God appears! He has the air of one who has a solemn work to do. There is gravity in his deportment, firmness in his countenance, and lightning in his eye. Unabashed by the myriad throng before him, undazzled by the splendid garments of the idol-serving priests, unappalled by the haughty mien of Ahab and his courtiers, he passes on, and takes his place over against his powerful adversaries. Alone he seems in that immense multitude, and yet he is not alone, for God is with him. So, pausing for a moment to survey the scene, he lifts up his voice like a trumpet, and throws down the gage of battle in these burning words: "How long halt ye between two opinions? If Jehovah be God, follow Him: but if Baal, then follow him."

To understand this appeal, we must remember that "the mass of the people, ignorant, and strongly addicted to idolatry, considered Baal as identical with Jehovah; while the worshippers of Jehovah, on the other hand, maintained His exclusive title to divine honours. The controversy, therefore, did not consist in a direct opposition between the worship of Jehovah and that of Baal; for the latter party, like the heathen in general, tolerated the worship of other deities, along with their own favourite idols; but, as Hengstenberg states it, 'the persecution was directed against those who, like Elijah, bore powerful testimony against the union of what was irreconcilable, and who loudly maintained that Jehovah identified with Baal was no longer Jehovah. The proposal which Elijah made from this point of view, that they should see whether Jehovah was God or Baal, the priests of Baal from their point of view understood to be, whether Jehovah-Baal was God, or Jehovah in perfect exclusiveness. The question that he put before making his proposal plainly implies that, in the popular opinion, these heterogeneous religious elements were blended in one.' " [1]

They at first made no answer to his pointed appeal. But as matters must be pushed to a decision, the prophet proposes that the whole thing should be settled by a sacrifice. The idolatrous prophets are to take a bullock, cut it in pieces, lay it on an altar, and put no fire under; Elijah is to do the same; they are to call upon Baal to consume their sacrifice; he is to call on Jehovah to consume his; "and the God which answereth by fire, let him be God."

The point of the proposal lay in this, that fire was the element over which Baal was believed by his

---

[1] "Commentary, Critical, Exegetical, and Practical," vol. ii. p. 354.

followers to have peculiar power. It was a bold offer, and one which, had he not been authorised of God, he would not have been justified in making ; but in the estimation of the people it was candid, fair, and honest, and they said, " It is well spoken."

The Baalites, we may suppose, would rather have backed out of it if they could have framed a feasible pretext for doing so, for they were all unprepared for an emergency like this. Their natural magic, their skill in sleight-of-hand, their dexterity in deceit, were useless when they were taken thus at unawares ; but Elijah knew what he was doing. He had counted on all this, and he had committed them before the multitude, just that they might have no opportunity to deceive, while at the same time they might have no good reason for asking delay. That nothing might be wanting on his side, he gives them the foremost place. They choose their bullock, dress it, lay it upon their altar, and wait the result. With loud cries they call upon their god, but "there is no voice, neither any that regardeth."

The noontide hour has come, yet still there is no sign ; and the sarcastic prophet, unable any longer to control his biting irony, says to them, " Cry aloud : for he is a god ; either he is talking, or he is pursuing, or he is in a journey, or peradventure he sleepeth, and must be awaked." Stung by his words, they leap in frantic devotion upon the altar, they cut themselves with knives and lancets till the blood gushed out upon them ;[1] and so they carry on until the time of the evening sacrifice, with no result.

---

[1] In his recent interesting and valuable book on " Bible Lands," Dr. Van-Lennep has the following passage illustrating

Most evidently, therefore, they have failed; but may it not be the same with Elijah, too? It is now his time. Let us see how he rises to the great occasion. Calling the people to come near unto him, he repairs an ancient altar to Jehovah, setting up twelve stones (for in such a solemn time he will not forget the essential unity of all the tribes), he digs a trench about it, puts the wood in order (mark, in order, for he is serving God, and he will do it right), he cuts the bullock in pieces, and lays them upon the wood; then three times he causes them to pour four barrels of water on the sacrifice, that it might be evident that there was no attempt to deceive; and when the time of the evening sacrifice is fully come, he bends himself in prayer.

And what a prayer he offers! brief, pointed, earnest, and believing, concentrating into few words the whole fire and fervour of his heart: " Jehovah, God of Abraham, Isaac, and of Israel, let it be known this day that Thou art God in Israel, and that I am

---

the self-torture of the Baalitish priests : " Our modern dervishes indulge in these practices only on special occasions, as, for instance, when a procession is organised and proceeds to the suburbs of a town to pray for rain, or for deliverance from some public calamity. They then exhibit some of their fanatical performances, calling upon God, and cutting themselves with knives and swords so that the blood runs, or piercing their almost naked bodies with wooden or iron spikes, from which they hang small mirrors. They sometimes become so exhausted with pain and loss of blood as to faint away, so that they have to be borne off." The same author gives two drawings taken from life, which enable us to form some idea of the revolting appearance of the priests of Baal on Mount Carmel.—See " Bible Lands," by Henry J. Van-Lennep, D.D., p. 767.

Thy servant, and that I have done all these things at Thy word. Hear me, O Jehovah, hear me, that this people may know that Thou art the Jehovah God, and that Thou hast turned their heart back again."

The train had been fully laid; every other preparation had been made; it needed only that it should thus be connected with Jehovah, and in a moment the fire descended, and "consumed the burnt-sacrifice, and the wood, and the stones, and the dust, and licked up the water that was in the trench."

Overawed by this manifestation of God's nearness to them, the multitudes fell on their faces and engaged for a brief space in silent homage; then, rising to their feet, they shouted again and again, "Jehovah, He is the God; Jehovah, He is the God." Meanwhile, consternation sits upon the countenances of the priests of Baal, and with bitter mortification in their hearts and fierce maledictions on their lips, they are led down to the river and slain with the sword.

While Ahab is keeping the sacrificial feast, the prophet is communing with God, and earnestly praying for rain; nor does he leave off until, after having been sent seven times, his servant came to tell him that a little cloud no bigger than a man's hand is rising out of the sea—the prelude of the coming answer to his cry. Thereafter he sent a message to Ahab to make haste and prepare his chariot, so that the rain might not retard his progress; and he himself, having tightened his girdle, and gathered his flowing mantle round his loins, ran on before the royal chariot, through the pelting torrent, to the palace gate. So ended this memorable day in the annals of Israel and in the history of man.

And now for the practical bearing of all this on us. Here, first, is brought before us the grand question which faces every man : " Who is your God—Baal, or Jehovah? sin, or the Holy One? self, or God? mammon, or Christ?" This is the question which each one of us has to settle for himself. It is needless to disguise the matter, or to shut our eyes to it, or to attempt to ignore it. This is the question which every man finds confronting him when he awakes to moral consciousness and responsibility, and which every day and every action calls upon him to solve. How have you solved it? I say, how have you solved it? for we have all given some answer to it already. Some have chosen to worship wealth, and, in their homage to that, everything else is neglected, or thought of only as it has a tendency to heap up gold. Some have chosen fame, and, at the sacrifice of ease and comfort, yea, by the most unscrupulous means, they seek to rise, and make for themselves a name among men. Some have said, " Intellect, be thou my god!" and they prostrate themselves before originality, so called, leaving the pillar of cloud and fire in revelation for the speculations of some would-be philosopher.

Others have found their God in sin, and, as their worship of it, have wallowed in the mire of sensuality and corruption. These be our modern Baal priests, albeit they wear no sacred vestments, nor bow the knee to any fairly fashioned image. Oh for another Elijah to summon them to another Carmel, that they may discover how miserably their gods will fail them in their hour of need!

But there are others who have chosen Jehovah as their God, and who, through good report and through evil report, have endeavoured to preserve their allegiance unto Him. Sometimes, indeed, they have been afraid to face the opposition of the great ones of the people, yet they have never bowed the knee before the popular Baal; and if they have erred at all, it has been by their silence, when they ought to have spoken out for Christ. Let them also come to Carmel, and see how, "when a man's ways please the Lord, He maketh even his enemies to be at peace with him." Let them learn " to be strong, and play the man for God," assured that He will not forsake those that put their trust in Him.

Others there are who, in fluctuating feeble-mindedness, endeavour to combine the services of Baal and Jehovah. When they are in one set of circumstances, as on the Lord's day, and in the church, they are for Jehovah. When they are in another set of circumstances, as on week-days, and in the transaction of their common business, they are for Baal, in one or other of his many forms. Yet how foolish, how weak, how vain, is an attempt like that! You might as well try to combine the eternal snow of the poles with the heat of the tropics, or to bring the East and the West together, or to make the darkness of midnight blend with the brightness of noonday, or to fill up that yawning chasm of infinite depth which for ever separates heaven from hell, as to try to weld together two such services as these. Nay, more, let all men know that even the attempt to combine the two is, after all, only serving Baal, and that in the meanest and most contemptible fashion. Jehovah, looking upon such a one, says, "I would thou wert cold or hot"; and Satan, beholding him, laughs at his simplicity, and inwardly chuckles at his own dexterity in leading his victim to destruction, by flattering him all the time that he is on the way to heaven.

If there be any such here, let me raise for them the old shout that woke the Carmel echoes: "How long leap ye between two opinions, as a bird leaps ever from twig to twig? If Jehovah be God, follow Him: but if Baal, then follow him. No man can serve two masters. Ye cannot serve God and Mammon. Choose ye this day whom ye will serve!" And, after what you have heard of His glory, who among you will refuse to say, "I will serve Jehovah"?

But we have here, secondly, the manner in which Jehovah manifested His claim to the sole allegiance of men. It was by accepted sacrifice. No thoughtful person can read this history without having vividly suggested to him a nobler Sacrifice, by a nobler Prophet. From the days of Cain and Abel downward, God seems to have challenged men to decide between the true religion and the false by means of sacrifice; and these priests and prophets of Baal, waiting all the day long, and crying, and cutting themselves with knives, are but the representatives of universal heathendom, vainly seeking, by sacrifices and penances, to propitiate their divinities.

Jehovah, in the history of the human race, like His servant here on this memorable day, allowed men to make their trial first. "But after that in the wisdom

of God the world by wisdom knew not God, it pleased
God, by the preaching of foolishness of preaching, to
save them that believe." [1]   When the fulness of the
time was come, and the hour of the world's evening
sacrifice had struck, "He sent forth His Son, made of
a woman, made under the law, to redeem them that
were under the law, that we might all receive the
adoption of sons " ; [2] and He laid Himself upon the
altar in the room of sinners, the Eternal Father
manifesting, by His resurrection from the dead, His
acceptance of the offering which He made on men's
behalf, even as here He showed His favour in the
descending fire.

What need we, therefore, any further controversy
on this great matter ?   Is not the resurrection of
Christ from the dead the best attested fact in human
history ?   And in the light of that fact, is not the
death of Christ a sufficient atonement for human
sin ?   Why need you bear the burden of your sin
longer?   See, it was already in the load which Jesus
"bore up to the cross, and left nailed to the accursed
tree.   Why need you seek by sufferings, or obedience
to make amends for your iniquities, when He has
borne your griefs and carried your sorrows? "

Here is the true, the only sacrifice for sin.   It has
been accepted by God, it needs only to be believingly
accepted by you—as offered on your behalf; and
then the Baalism of your hearts will be slain as
effectively by Jesus' love, as the priests were
slaughtered here by Elijah's sword.   Ah ! if you will
only learn the real meaning of the cross of Christ,

[1] 1 Cor. i. 21.   [2] Gal. iv. 4, 5.

and accept Him as your Redeemer, there will be no longer any question in your hearts as to the service of Jehovah. You will not be able to keep from serving Him, for the impulse of your souls will be to say that you are not your own, but "bought with a price," and therefore bound to "glorify Him in your bodies, and your spirits, which are His."

From Carmel, then, I lead you to Calvary, that in the sacrifice offered thereon by Jesus Christ for the sins of men you may see the atonement for your sins; and that in the empty sepulchre of Joseph you may see the pledge of your resurrection to newness of life with Christ, and, at the last, to glorified humanity with Himself. Oh, if, as he looked upon the meek majesty of the Holy Sufferer, the Roman Centurion was constrained to say, "Truly this was the Son of God;" if, as the doubting apostle beheld the print of the nails in His hands, and the mark of the spear-gash in His side, he exclaimed, in the startled ejaculation of adoring faith, "My Lord and my God"; surely, as we contemplate the whole significance of that death upon the cross, and that resurrection from the grave, we ought to cry, Jehovah-Jesus, He is the God! Jehovah-Jesus, He is the God! Him will we serve, and His voice will we obey.

Finally, let us observe, that the question as to who our God shall be is one of immediate urgency. The appeal is, "How long halt ye between two opinions?" Undecided hearer, what are you waiting for? Are you wishing better evidence than that which has been furnished you? Then you will never receive any stronger testimony than that which was given here, or on Calvary and in the garden; and if you reject that, we must say regarding you, Neither will you be persuaded if one came unto you directly from the grave. If you think that insufficient, then there must be some other reason than a lack of evidence that leads you to be undecided. The cause may be a moral one, and there may be some secret sin holding you fast in the meshes of its invisible threads, or some hidden lust to which you are wedded, or some unseen idol that you are really worshipping; and in that case you have already, for all your apparent indecision, determined to reject God; that is, you have, for the gratification of your lusts, made up your minds to act as if it were a settled thing that the Bible is a lie, and that God is non-existent.

Or perhaps the cause may be intellectual, and you may be insisting on a kind of proof which cannot be furnished to you on any moral question. The truth of the Bible cannot be established by a demonstration like that by which you reach a conclusion in a mathematical problem. And to insist upon evidence of such a sort in its behalf betrays on your part a mental defect or an intellectual mistake. You have to be content here with moral certainty ; you have to accept here, not one abstract demonstration, but the sum total of a great variety of separate testimonies, all of them converging to one point, and making, by their cumulative force, an incontrovertible impression on the candid mind.

But there is a third possibility that presents itself. Perhaps you are waiting, that it may be easier for you to declare yourself. That is, you will tarry till you discover which is the popular side, and to that you will adhere. But how unmanly is a course like that ! What signifies it whether the majority be with you or not; if only you are right, you are always in the majority, for you have God on your side. Shame on you to wait for personal considerations when truth and right and God are concerned.

There is a battle raging on the earth between good and evil, between God and Satan, between Christ and antichrist; and it is cowardly in the extreme for you to linger on the outskirts of the field, shrouded in the smoke that is issuing from the conflict, and waiting only till victory declares itself, that then you may come down and claim the honours of a triumph which you did nothing to win.

Come forth, and quit yourselves like men in this great fight. Take the one side or the other; and, oh, take the side of the Lord Jesus Christ! Fight the good fight of faith, and so lay hold on eternal life. The matter is urgent. Make haste; for, if you delay much longer, death may decide it for you, and fix you everlastingly among the foes of God.

Wavering sinner, you are, so to say, in the twilight; but it rests with you to determine whether it shall be the twilight of the morning, brightening into the full splendour of heaven's own eternal noonday, or that of the evening, darkening down into the blackness of hell's own endless night. To the one or to the other it must come at last. Halt no longer, therefore, but decide for God through Jesus Christ our Lord; and by the help of His Holy Spirit, slay every Baalitish principle within you.

> " Then bright as morning shall come forth
> In peace and joy thy days ;
> And glory from the Lord above
> Shall shine on all thy ways."

VII.

PRAYER AND ITS ANSWER.

1 KINGS xviii. 40–46.

THE slaughter of the prophets of Baal, at the
command of Elijah, immediately after his sacrifice on Mount Carmel had been consumed by fire
from heaven, has been by many regarded as a high-
handed proceeding, and the enemies of the Bible
have not hesitated to cry out against it as both
immoral and inhuman.

In answer to all such allegations, however, it might
be enough to say that the destruction of the idolatrous prophets must be·taken in connection with the
whole events of the day. We are not warranted
to view it by itself alone, but we must look upon it as
the sequel of the miraculous acceptance of Elijah's
sacrifice by fire; which not only proved that Jehovah
was God, but also that Elijah was His duly accredited
servant. Hence the order of Elijah was virtually the
command of God, who has the right to take away the
lives which men by their sins have forfeited, whensoever and howsoever He pleases. If the reality of the
miracle be disproved, then we may charge Elijah with
cruelty, though in that case it would be hard to see
how he, acting alone, could so move the people as to

persuade them to carry out his instructions.   If, on the other hand, the reality of the miracle be granted, we must hold that Elijah in issuing his command was acting in the name and by the authority of God.

But this, in the estimation of some tender and sensitive spirits, may only seem to aggravate the difficulty.   They could conceive of Elijah, a man of like passions with other men, acting after the fashion here described, for no prophet was infallible in his character ; but they find it hard to believe that God, who is, according to the Apostle John, love itself, should countenance and encourage, far less command, such a proceeding as that which is here described.

But, in reply to all this, we would remind objectors that love is by no means inconsistent with the execution of a penalty on those who have violated a righteous law.   Love to the criminal in the remission of his sentence is cruelty and injustice to the nation. To pardon a thief, for example, and let him loose upon society to renew his dishonesty, might be regarded by some as kindness to him, but it is the greatest unkindness to the community.

Now, in the nation of Israel, God was the real king, and each occupant of the throne on earth was required to rule in harmony with a certain written code of laws.   These laws are contained in the Books of Moses, and among them are the most stringent statutes against idolatry.   That among the Israelites was not merely an immoral thing, as it is and must be everywhere, but it was also a crime ; that is, an offence against the law of the nation, and a dishonour to Him who was its real king.   These prophets of Baal, therefore, by introducing a new divinity into the land, were guilty not only of sin against the God of heaven, but also of high treason, and so as traitors they had forfeited their lives.

Besides, the idolatry which they were mainly instrumental in producing brought as its punishment temporal calamities upon the people ; and as these could be removed only by the abolition of the idolatry, love to the nation as a whole demanded that they should be destroyed.

This execution must be regarded as having occurred under a theocracy ; and when we so view it, we see at once how it was perfectly justifiable in such circumstances, while it would be utterly unjustifiable in the times in which we live. Idolatry was then a crime as well as a sin. Now, it is a sin only, and as such, it is not within the province of any government to deal with it ; but the person who is guilty of it must be held as answerable to God alone.

Nor has any ruler in the Christian church the right to imitate Elijah here. He was a prophet of the old covenant, and as such was bound to act in accordance with the laws of Moses. The office-bearer in the Church is a ruler, under the new covenant, of a spiritual society, and is under obligations to rule only in accordance with the precepts of Christ and the principles laid down by His apostles. Now, among these there is no warrant for the use of the sword. The power which the Christian office-bearer wields is that of truth, and if the truth which he proclaims be by men rejected, they must be left to be dealt with by God Himself. It is important thus to distinguish between things that differ, and to show how a vindica-

tion of Elijah here does not involve the approval of
persecution now for religious or irreligious belief.

After this terrible sentence had been executed in
the valley beside the river Kishon, Elijah said unto
Ahab, "Get thee up; eat and drink, for there is a
sound of abundance of rain;" and the king, with the
bitterness of defeat within his heart, reascended the
hill, and sat down to the feast which was always
associated with the offering of sacrifice.

While he and his courtiers were thus engaged,
Elijah, with his servant, who now for the first time
appears in the narrative, went still farther up the
mountain. Taking his station in a fit place of retreat,
the prophet gave himself to pray, and sent his servant
to the summit to watch the result, away out on the
Mediterranean Sea.

Now concerning this supplication of Elijah's a few
things need to be said.

In the first place, it is somewhat remarkable that
he offered prayer at all. He had said to Ahab that
there was a sound of abundance of rain; he had also
affirmed, three years and a half before, that the rain
would come at his own word. What need, then, one
is inclined to ask, for prayer at all? Might he not
have spoken the word just at the moment? But no!
Elijah knew, what it behoves us also to remember,
that the fulfilment of God's promises comes in the
way of answers to prayer. He knew that to every
prediction of blessing the condition is annexed, "For
this will I be inquired of to do it for you;" and so
he gave himself to prayer. He believed that to be
a law of God's moral government, as imperative and
unchanging as any of those in the physical universe,

of which, in these days, so much is said; and therefore he set himself to earnest supplication.

Again, it is noteworthy that Elijah withdrew from
all society when he prayed. He went up to be alone;
and he did so in order that the full strength of his
fervent soul might be given to the work in which he
was engaging. Yes, I say the *work;* for Elijah's
prayer was no mere form, neither was it the calm
musing of a meditative spirit; but it was the earnest
wrestling of one whose intellect, and heart, and will,
and conscience were all vigorously exercised for the
production of the result at which he aimed.

When, on one occasion, the Lord Jesus was praying, we are informed that, when He ceased, His disciples came unto Him, and requested to be taught
to pray. Now, the word there rendered "ceased"
literally means when He "rested," implying that
prayer with Christ, as with Elijah, was a work in which
the whole soul was engaged. It was a saying of
Bishop Hamilton of Salisbury, and is quoted by
Canon Liddon, that "no man was likely to do much
good in prayer who did not begin by looking upon
it in the light of a work to be prepared for and per-
severed in with all the earnestness which we bring to
bear upon subjects which are, in our opinion, at once
most interesting and most necessary."[1] Ah, how far
from this is it too frequently with us! We are list-
less, indifferent, formal, cold. So far from having
our whole souls in active exertion, we are too frequently utterly uninterested in our own devotions,
using expressions by rote, and going over petitions as

---

[1] "Some Elements of Religious Thought," p. 172.

mechanically as the little figures in a Swiss clock go through their hourly exercises. Let us Elijah-like, concentrate ourselves on the great work of supplication ; and soon we, too, shall have answers such as those which he enjoyed.

Further, we are impressed with the fact that Elijah here had a definite object in view when he prayed. Too often even professing Christians go to their knees with no distinct purpose shaped within their souls. They have been taught to believe that it is their duty to pray, and so they go into their closets to perform a duty. They use certain stereotyped phrases, which have come down, as it were, by tradition from the fathers, and form part of all orthodox prayers; they ask for things which they ought to desire, rather than for those which they really at the moment wish ; and thus the exercises which were meant to be a joy and refreshment to the spirit become a burden and a weariness. Let us see to it, therefore, that we pause and consider what we are going to ask before we begin to pray.

It would be a good thing, indeed, as helping to produce this concentration of heart, if we were to write distinctly down before our own eyes that which it was our intention to ask from God. Elijah would not here have been taken aback if he had been asked, " What did you request from God ?" His whole soul was bent on securing rain. He had done all he could in the way of purging the land from idolatry; and he now turned to God to remove the curse which for idolatry was resting on the land. He knew what he wanted. Yet what confusion would often cover us if, after we have risen from our knees some one were to ask us, "What have you been praying for?"

Look at the prayer offered by Elijah before the fire came down and consumed the sacrifice; look at the prayers offered by Moses, by Daniel, by Nehemiah, and others, as they have been preserved in this book, and see how definite they were. They went to the object which the suppliants had in view as straight as an arrow to its mark ; and we shall never pray aright until we learn this definiteness.

If one, in his daily business, should go to a fellow-merchant, and present a request with the same circumlocution which is too often used in prayer, or if he should indulge in the same pointless generalities which are so common in our petitions, he would be laughed to scorn, and would be counted anything but earnest.   Brethren, let us reform this altogether, and be as natural and direct in our requests to God as our children are in their applications to us.

Notice, again, how Elijah expected an answer to his prayer.   He sent his servant to the summit to look out for its appearance.   He regarded it as a certainty that the answer would come ; and just as when you have written to a dear friend asking advice on some important matter, it never occurs to you to doubt that he will answer, and you watch for the postman every morning to see whether the reply has come, so it never entered into Elijah's mind to doubt that his prayer would be granted.   The strangest of all things to him would have been that his prayer should be unanswered.   So he set a watch for the coming of the answer.

Now, how different all this is from our procedure, I

need hardly stay to show. Is it not true that we
speak of answers to prayer as almost unwonted
things? When one of our own prayers is answered,
we cannot think enough of it; and this not so much
because of God's kindness in giving it—for that would
be well enough—as because of its unusualness in our
experience. The wonder is to us that our prayer has
been answered at all.

Take up a book of religious anecdotes, and you
will probably see a section headed thus : " Remarkable Answers to Prayer;" but what unbelief is there
in the very title ! Why, that real prayer should be
answered by God for Jesus' sake is not a remarkable
thing; it is one of the laws of His spiritual government that such prayer should be answered, and the
wonderful thing would be if, after the promises He has
made, He were to ignore our petitions. Is it, after
all, so remarkable a thing that God should keep His
promise? If He were a frail, erring man, who had
often broken His word, and had obtained the reputation of being untruthful, it might be something astonishing if, on one or two occasions, He should keep
His promise. But He is the faithful God, and the
wonder is that we should be surprised at any manifestation of His faithfulness.

Brethren, there is an immense amount of unbelief
underlying the common modes of speech even of
professing Christians on this subject. It is not
singular that God should hear prayer; but, oh ! it is
singular that, with so many of His promises plainly
given us in His Word, and with the manifestation of
His love to us in the cross of His Son before our eyes,
we should not calculate upon His answering our

prayers just as we do upon the response of a beloved
friend to the earnest letter which we have sent him
for sympathy and advice.

Elijah would have been surprised if God had not
answered him; we, alas! in our unbelief, are surprised when He does answer us! Let us have done
with all this; and when we direct our prayer unto
God, let us look up, expecting some result.

I remark, again, that Elijah was importunate in his
prayer. Six times the servant whom he had stationed
on the hill-top returned with the reply, "There is
nothing;" but that did not dishearten the prophet.
He kept on at his prayer; he knocked again and
again, until the response was given.

Nor is this a solitary instance of believing impor-
tunity in petition. Jesus, in Gethsemane, threw Himself three times upon the earth praying the same
words. Paul besought the Lord thrice that his thorn
in the flesh might be removed. The Syrophenician
woman clung to Christ, and would not let Him go
until the blessing came. From these cases let us
learn not to be disappointed if at first no answer
comes. Though it tarry, wait for it; it will surely
come—it will not tarry; "and of this let us be sure,
that no true prayer is ever lost." Either in spirit or
in letter, it will be surely answered. The God of
heaven has promised to hear His children's cry, and
His throne shall totter, and Himself cease to be the
ruler of the world, sooner than His word shall be
falsified or His pledge broken.

Finally, here, Elijah recognised the answer when it
came, for when the seventh time his servant came,
saying, " Behold, there ariseth a little cloud out of

the sea, like a man's hand," he saw in this the response to his prayer, and sent a message to Ahab to hasten his departure, lest the rain should hinder his return to his palace.

Some have taken this as an illustration of the gradual manner in which God often answers His people's prayers, and sends His blessings; but I confess that, to me, there is nothing that suggests the gradual in the description that is here given, for the fact that the king was bid to make haste shows rather that the storm came on at once in all its force.

But while I do not see that idea in the narrative before me, I think we have here an indication of the fact that God answers His people's prayers through the ordinary operations of the laws of nature. There was nothing in the coming of this storm different from the rising of those which are common in the eastern portion of the Mediterranean. That this is the case is clear from the statements made by modern voyagers in the Levant.

"Of several instances which occur to us," says Dr. Kitto,[1] "the most graphic is that given by Mr. Emerson, in his 'Letters from the Ægean.' He is at sea in a Greek vessel in the Levant. One morning, which had opened clear and beautiful, it was announced that a squall might be expected. No sign recognisable by European landsmen appeared; but on attention being properly directed, 'a little black cloud was seen on the verge of the horizon toward the scuth, which was every instant spreading rapidly over the face of the sky, and drawing nearer to the

---

[1] "Daily Bible Illustrations," vol. iv. p. 272.

vessel. Order was immediately given to strike sail, and to prepare the vessel for scudding before the hurricane. But scarcely an instant had elapsed ere the squall was upon us, and all grew black around; the wind came swishing and crisping over the water, and in a moment the ship was running almost gunwale down, while the rain was dashing in torrents on the decks.' Mr. Emerson adds, that it is mainly the dread of such sudden bourrasques that compels almost every vessel in the Levant to shorten sail at the close of day, since it would be next to impossible during the night to discern the cloud which announces the approach of the tempest in time to prepare for its reception, and to a ship with all her canvas spread the effect might be terrific."

Thus, then, Elijah's prayer was answered through the operation of God's ordinary laws for the regulation of the forces of nature; and so we have in this a triumphant reply to those who assert that the hearing of prayer by God must involve an interference with the laws of nature which would amount to a miracle. For there is no word here of miracle; and the storm came that evening precisely as storms come in that region yet. Hence we are shut up to the inference that this prayer was answered through God's usual channels of operation, and we must conclude that what men call physical laws have been arranged by God with the view of His carrying on through them the course of His providence, and answering by them the prayers of His people. How this has been accomplished, I cannot tell; that it is the case, I am forced to conclude, not only from this narrative, but also from many others in this sacred Book.

But some one may say : " Not so fast! If this storm came only as other storms come, through the operation of natural laws, how can you hold that Elijah's prayer was answered by its coming? May there not be here only a coincidence ? "

Now, to this I reply, that if we had nothing more before us than the fact that a man prayed for rain, and the other fact that the rain came just after he had prayed, we might say that there was only a coincidence ; but we have more than these two things to contemplate. We have to take in, besides, the truth that God has promised to hear prayer, and the fact that Elijah offered his prayer in the faith of that promise ; and when we include these, it is impossible any longer to speak of coincidence.

A friend promises to another that, if he will let him know when he is in need, he will be always ready to help him. The hour of need comes. He writes for help, and by the first post thereafter his friend, availing himself of the ordinary channels of communication, sends a letter enclosing money. Is this any the less an answer to prayer because the benevolent man used the regular means of transmitting his gift, and did not send a special messenger with it by an unusual route? or does the recipient in such a case speak of mere coincidence ? No ; but he sees the fulfilment of a promise, and rejoices in the new assurance which he has received of the faithfulness of his friend. Just so here. We must have regard to the promise of God, and the suppliant's faith in it, as well as to the coming of that which the suppliant prays for ; and when we bring these in, it is the merest absurdity to speak of a coincidence.

I know that just now it is the fashion, in certain scientific quarters, to deny the possibility of prayers being ever answered, and to deride the very offering of it; but these philosophers forget, on the one hand, the natural impulse of the burdened heart to pray, and, on the other, the promise which God has given to answer prayer. "There are more things in heaven and earth" than they have dreamed of, or can understand. When God created the world, He certainly did not shut Himself out of it; and He who gave the universe its laws can surely so employ them as to answer the entreaties of His children through them. To suppose the contrary is to degrade the Almighty below the level of a common artificer, and to make Him the slave, and not the master, of the elements of nature.

Some time ago, being at Binghamton, in this State, I went to see the machinery wherewith that city is supplied with water. In a small house on the bank of the Susquehanna, there is an engine, which goes night and day, pumping water into the mains. The demand for water acts as a governor on the engine, and regulates its motion, so that the more water is drawn off, the faster the engine goes. Then, when a fire occurs, an alarm-bell is rung, on hearing which the engineer gears on some extra machinery, which causes the engine to move more rapidly, and charges the ordinary mains to their fullest capacity, so that they can send water through the hose to the top of the highest building in the place. Now, if men can thus construct an engine whereby, through ordinary and already existing channels, an emergency of prayer may be met, why cannot God do the same in this machine which we call the universe? As we understand the matter, it is thus He does proceed. He uses His natural laws for the carrying forward of His purposes in grace, and for the help of His believing children ; and, as Isaac Taylor has suggestively said, "the greatest miracle of God's providence is that it is carried on without miracle," while yet it makes provision for the answering of prayer, and for the accomplishment of the great purpose of the Divine Mind.

But I must hasten on to the conclusion of the narrative. As the storm began, Ahab mounted his chariot and rode on toward Jezreel, while Elijah, under a divine impulse, girded his loins and ran before him to the gate of the palace. I have seen no explanation of this apparently strange procedure at all equal to that given by Dr. Thomson in "The Land and the Book ;" and as it would only mar the beauty of his statement if I were to attempt either to paraphrase or to abridge it, I shall content myself with simply reproducing his words :

"This," says that excellent writer, "has always seemed to me most extraordinary conduct for a man of Elijah's age, character, and office. And yet, when rightly understood, it was beautiful and full of important instruction. Elijah, as God's minister, had overwhelmed the king with shame and confusion in the presence of his subjects. The natural tendency of this would be to lower him in their eyes, and lessen their respect for his authority. It was not the intention, however, to weaken the government, nor to encourage rebellion. The prophet was, therefore, divinely directed to give a testimony of respect and honour to the king as public and striking as from necessity had been the opposition and rebuke to his idolatry. The mode of doing honour to Ahab by running before his chariot was in accordance with the customs of the East even to this day. I was reminded of this incident more than twenty years ago, at Jaffa, when Mohammed Ali came to that city with a large army to quell the rebellion of Palestine. The camp was on the sandhills south of the city, while Mohammed Ali stopped inside the walls. The officers were constantly coming and going, preceded by runners, who always kept just ahead of the horses, no matter how furiously they were ridden; and in order to run with the greater ease, they not only girded their loins very tightly, but also tucked up their loose garments under the girdle, lest they should be incommoded by them. Thus, no doubt, did Elijah. The distance from the base of Carmel across the plain to Jezreel is not less than twelve miles; and the race was probably accomplished in two hours, in the face of a tremendous storm of rain and wind. It was necessary that the hand of the Lord should be upon the prophet, or he would not have been able to achieve it." [1]

We have, all through this evening's lecture, set ourselves to give a practical direction to the example of the prophet, and so we may be the more readily excused if we shall, for once, finish with a doctrinal deduction. In our last discourse we spoke of the sacrifice on Mount Carmel as having been, in some sort, typical of the greater offering by a greater pro-

---

[1] "The Land and the Book," English edition, p. 485.

phet on Calvary ; and it surely cannot be unnatural if we connect the prayer of Elijah with its answer in the wind and rain, with the descent of the Holy Spirit upon the infant Church on Pentecost, in answer to the continuous supplications of the first disciples.

The sacrifice of Christ, valuable as it was, was not all that was needed for the world's salvation. The descent of the Spirit was just as needful as the offering of Himself upon the cross by Jesus. The one without the other would have been of no avail. By the union of both the salvation of the believing soul is effected. The cross was the magnet, but the Spirit is the hand that holds that magnet, and draws men's souls to God. The cross is the great instrumentality by which the soul is renewed and sanctified and made meet for heaven ; but the Spirit is the agent who makes that instrumentality effectual. Just as in the present instance, though Elijah had overcome the idolaters in securing the acceptance of his sacrifice, the land would still have remained parched and barren had there been no rain ; so, even after the death of Christ on Calvary, and His resurrection from the tomb of Joseph, the world would have remained to a large extent unblessed had there been no succeeding Pentecost.

Thus we may see how much we owe to these hundred and twenty suppliants in the upper room who continued instant in prayer, until, with the sound as of a tempest, the Spirit of fire descended on them, to purify and consecrate them for the Master's work, and to clothe them with power from on high for its prosecution.

Nor is this true only in regard of Christ's sacrifice

as related to Pentecost. It is as true yet of the preaching of Christ crucified and its relation to the conversion of men. It is not enough that we have a faithful minister who sets forth before the eyes of his hearers Jesus Christ, evidently crucified for them. That of itself will not convert them, and cause the verdure of the new life to spring up within their souls. The heavenly rain of the Spirit is required for that as well as the preaching of the Cross.

Let us never forget this. Let the minister retire from his pulpit as Elijah went here to his closet, and let the hearers do the same ; let them together plead that God would send down His Spirit in rich effusion; let them be earnest, believing, and importunate in their prayers ; and then there will be " a sound of abundance of rain." Souls will be converted, the Church will be revived, the neighbourhood will be blessed, and anew the old oracles will be fulfilled. " The wilderness and the solitary place shall be glad for them ; the desert shall rejoice and blossom as the rose." " He shall come unto us as the rain, as the latter and former rain unto the earth." " He shall come down like rain upon the mown grass, and as showers that water the earth." To your knees, then, my hearers, to your knees ! Go, beseech God to pour out His Spirit upon us all; and who can tell but that from this evening service there shall commence a blessing which shall be like a new Pentecost to all our souls, and the effects of which shall radiate from us until all around are made to own the reality and to feel the power of the Redeemer's grace ? Would to God that it might be so indeed !

VIII.

UNDER THE JUNIPER-TREE.

1 KINGS xix. 1-18.

WHEN Ahab returned to Jezreel, and reported to Jezebel the proceedings on Mount Carmel, with their disastrous issue for the priests of Baal, her rage knew no bounds. She thought of Elijah as her only adversary, and, tracing the whole effect to some trickery or sleight-of-hand of his, she sent to him a message of revengeful import : "So let the gods do to me, and more also, if I make not thy life as the life of one of them by to-morrow about this time." She refused to acknowledge the sovereignty of Jehovah, even when proved by such convincing signs as those which Elijah had given, and she vainly imagined that if she could only destroy the prophet's life, she would also annihilate the cause with which he was identified. She had not been herself on Carmel a spectator of the descending fire upon Elijah's sacrifice; and, with the true spirit of the sceptic, who will not believe the eyes of others, and, unless it suits his own purposes, will not believe his own, she would not acknowledge that any miracle had been wrought. "It was all a delusion. By some premonitory indications, Elijah knew that the drought

was about to cease, and, calculating on the coming
thunder-storm, he thought he could make the people
believe that the wood upon his altar was kindled by
fire from heaven, whereas it was only a flash of lightning; and as for the rain coming as the result of his
prayer, that was all a superstition—it was a mere
coincidence—only that, and nothing more; and
when the morning dawned, she would turn the tables
upon him, and make sure that he, at least, would
never again interfere with Ahab's plan for the Baal-
ising of the kingdom of Israel."

Had she been merely fighting with a man, she
might have succeeded; but Elijah was only the
servant of Jehovah, and though he were removed,
Jehovah would remain as omnipotent as ever. This
is forgotten by all persecutors of the faith; and in
reference to every kind of religious intolerance, the
advice of Gamaliel may well be pondered by the
governments that practise it: "Refrain from these
men, and let them alone: for if this counsel or this
work be of men, it will come to naught: but if it be
of God, ye cannot overthrow it; lest haply ye be
found even to fight against God." [1]

When Elijah heard what Jezebel had said, a sudden
panic seized him, and he arose and fled for his life,
resting not until he came to Beer-sheba, the southern
extremity of Judah. But he would not remain even
in that utmost border of the land; for though the
good Jehoshaphat was then king at Jerusalem, his
son had married the daughter of Jezebel, and, in his
paroxysm of terror, the prophet would not stay where

---

[1] Acts v. 38, 39.

any of the kin of Ahab had any influence whatever.
So, leaving his servant at Beer-sheba, he went a full
day's journey into the wilderness, and flung himself
at even-tide under the lee of a shrub, here called a
juniper-tree. "It was a white-blossomed broom,
abundant in Spain, Barbary, Syria, and the desert of
Sinai, and known in British shrubberies as the Spanish
Broom."[1] Dr. Bonar, in his account of his journey
through Sinai, describing a bush of this species, says :
"It was under this tree that Elijah sat down to take
shelter from the heat, and more than once did we do
the same ; for some of these shrubs are bushy and
tall, perhaps eight or ten feet high. They formed a
shadow, sometimes from the heat, sometimes from
the wind, and sometimes from the rain, both for man
and beast. It was about the best shadow that the
desert could afford, save when we could get under
some great rock or shaggy palm."[2]

Under such a broom-bush, then, in his fear, his
weariness, his self-reproach, and his despair, Elijah
threw himself, and requested that he might die, saying, "It is enough ; now, O Lord, take away my life ;
for I am not better than my fathers." Is this the
man who had bearded Ahab in his court; whose
prayer had sealed and opened heaven, whose faith
had raised the dead, and who had put to confusion
the prophets of Baal on the brow of Carmel? Is this
he who heretofore has never feared the face of man ?
Is this Elijah the Tishbite, fleeing from death, and
yet with almost maniacal inconsistency supplicating

---

[1] Fairbairn's "Imperial Bible Dictionary :" article *Juniper-tree.*
[2] Bonar's "Sinai," p. 196.

for death ? Alas, it is even so ! "The best of men are but men at the best." Grand and noble as he was, he was, after all, only "a man of like passions with ourselves ;" and in this panic-stricken paralysis of his faith there is as much to instruct us as in his bold denunciation of the wrong, and manly struggle for the right. It seems, indeed, a strange collapse ; yet I am not sure but that most of us will have more affinity with him as he lies here in his dark depression than as he stood that other day in his reforming might, calling the thousands of Israel to decision. Paul, in his peculiar experiences, has taught us that when we are weak then we may be strong. To-night we may learn, from the fugitive prophet under the juniper-tree, that where we are strong, there we may be weak. Let us try if we can in any degree account for this unusual conduct on Elijah's part, and let us also carefully follow God's dealing with him in the despondency out of which his conduct grew.

In speaking of the causes of Elijah's sudden depression, I would, like Robertson, of Brighton— whose sermon on this chapter[1] has well-nigh swept the whole field of thought on the subject, and left the merest handful to all after-gleaners—give prominence to the physical reaction which must have followed upon the intense excitement of the previous days. In our complex humanity there is a mysterious sympathy between the body and the spirit. When the mind is earnestly engaged, it gives, for the time, its vigour and energy to the body ; so that we are not surprised to hear of John Knox, that in his last days he had to be supported into the pulpit

---

[1] Robertson's "Sermons," Second Series, p. 95.

by a servant on each side of him, and behooved to lean upon it at his first entry ; but, as James Melville says, " er he had done with his sermone, he was so active and so vigorous that he was lyk to ding the pulpit in blads (knock the pulpit to pieces), and flie out of it." But, on the other hand, when, after long-continued tension, the strain is slackened, and the body is run down, it imparts its weariness to the spirit.

In the heat of a man's enthusiastic devotion to some pursuit, and while the absolute necessity for exertion is upon him, he is not conscious of physical fatigue ; but when the work is done, and the weight of responsibility removed, both body and mind sink into a state of weakness which makes every thought of exertion a distress. In such a condition the slightest noise will seem to sound as with the report of a revolver, and every call to attention will rasp upon the nervous system with an agony, the intensity of which can be understood only by those who have felt it. The natural equipoise of the system has been disturbed ; and as, when you take a weight out of the one scale on the balance, the other sinks at once to a depth corresponding to the height to which the first rises, so when, by some anxious and harassing exertion, a man has been held long on a stretch, the moment the work is finished there will come a rebound into a state of weakness which is as far below the usual condition of his system as his former strength was above it.

When a mother, or a sister, or a wife is watching by the bedside of a dear one, a marvellous power of endurance is evoked, sleep and rest seem almost unnecessary, and for the time the nurse is a wonder to herself and all around her. But when the danger is past, and the patient has recovered, then there is a recoil, and the effects of the over-exertion of a few weeks tell for months, both upon the body and the mind. The valley is as deep as the mountain is high. The ebb of the tide is proportioned to its height; and is ever greatest when the flood-tide has been at the spring. So excessive tension of our bodily system will induce as excessive relaxation, and that, in its turn, will tell upon the tone of the mind. This is the law of our human nature. We all understand it; we have all experienced it; and we must give Elijah here the full benefit of it. Think what we had gone through during these preceding few days of exciting toil. After his challenge to the priests of Baal, there was the earnestness of his prayerful preparation for the encounter; then there was the long day of actual conflict on the mountain; then his wrestling with God for the rain; and then his rapid race before Ahab's chariot all the way from Carmel to Jezreel. Now, all these coming one upon another, must have worn out even so muscular a frame as Elijah's; for observe there was much more than mere physical toil.

Everybody knows that there is nothing so exhaustive as deep emotion. Now, the conflict on the mountain stirred the prophet's heart to its depths, and prayer like his must itself have been a labour of the most fatiguing kind. Hence, when the threat of Jezebel was repeated to him, and he saw no attempt made by the people to rally round him, we can easily understand how, in the state of prostration to which he was reduced, his faith failed him, and he turned and fled. Had he better understood the demands of his own frame upon him, he might probably have struggled more manfully against this physical reaction; and might have reasoned that Jezebel was no more dangerous to him now than she had been before. But, in his ignorance of the cause of his depression, he magnified the peril in which he stood, while at the same time he forgot the faithfulness of that protector who before had hidden him in the valley of the Cherith and the cottage of Zarephath. Let us learn, therefore, from his case not to mistake the lassitude of the body for the desertion of Jehovah. Many of our darkest hours are caused not so much by spiritual evils as by physical derangements. And not seldom we apply to God's ministers for religious consolation, when we should repair to our physician for medical treatment.

But another cause of Elijah's depression is to be found in the fact that he had been thus far companionless. By this I do not mean that he had stood alone in the land, without the encouragement of knowing that at least seven thousand had been faithful to Jehovah, but rather that he had found no intimate human friend who could soothe him by personal sympathy and affection. It is no doubt true that there is a certain solitariness about every man, and that the greater the man is, the greater is his loneliness. Nor do I forget that when one can get access to God in prayer, the lack of human confidential friendship is more than compensated. Still, there is a craving in every heart for earthly companionship; nay, more, there is a healing power in such fellowship which tends to refresh our hearts and keep us from depression. He who formed us said, "It is not good for man to be alone," and in the companionship of a wife—when a man has the wisdom to make her a companion, and not a mere ornamental appendix to himself—there is great moral benefit.

The beautiful myth of English history tells how Queen Eleanor sucked the poison out of her husband's wounds ; and in a moral and spiritual sense this is what every true-hearted wife seeks to do. She takes the poison from the wounds which her husband receives in the daily battle of life. This, also, in a lower degree indeed, but yet in a very great degree, is what a real friend does for his friend ; and if Elijah here had but possessed such a companion, he might have been saved from his flight into the wilderness. Up till this time, however, his solitariness had been the great blank of his life. He had been a Luther without his Melancthon; a Peter without his John ; a Calvin without his Beza.

It is instructive to note how, almost in all ages and lands, God has sent out his reformers as at first Christ sent His evangelists, two by two, that the weakness of the one might, in some measure, be supplemented by the strength of the other. But Elijah had no one to consult with ; no one to speak to him of his nervous prostration and exaggerated fears ; no one to take for a moment, as it were, the lever of his thoughts, and switch them off upon a different track ; and so he ran away. Perhaps, during his past career, he had undervalued human society, wrapping himself up in solemn exclusiveness, not courting or caring for a friend; but now he suffers for this lack ; and it is not without significance as tending to confirm this view, that almost immediately after, Elisha was associated with him as his coadjutor and companion.

Let us learn from all this, therefore, to cultivate some special friendship which may prove a solace to us in time of trouble. We do ourselves injustice, and prepare for ourselves collapse, and defeat like this of Elijah, when we keep ourselves aloof, frowning down all advances on the part of those who desire to be our friends, and determining to stand alone. Ah, how have I seen the strong man bowed down and lying wailing under the juniper-tree, because, by his exclusiveness and reticence, he had in former times so surrounded himself with *chevaux-de-frise* that no one could get near him with sympathy and succour! The wise man here may well instruct us: "Two are better than one ; because they have a good reward for their labour. For if they fall, the one will lift up his fellow : but woe to him that is alone when he falleth. And if one prevail against him, two shall withstand him ; and a threefold cord is not quickly broken." [1]

Still another cause for Elijah's depression may, perhaps, be found in the exaggerated expectations which he had been cherishing in regard to the results of his work. That thrilling cheer which made the echoes ring on Carmel, when the people shouted, " Jehovah, He is the God ; Jehovah, He is the God," had been interpreted by him as meaning that the

---

[1] Ecclesiastes iv. 9, 10, 12.

subjects of Ahab would at once abjure idolatry, and
rally round him as the prophet of Jehovah. But
now, when Jezebel threatened his life, and no voice
is raised on his behalf, he is disappointed and seeks
the wilderness. He imagines that his work has been
in vain, and that the purpose of his life has been
lost. His labour, he thinks, has been like water
spilt upon the ground ; and so, in deepest self-
abasement, he comes to God, saying, " Why should
I live any longer? I wanted to stem the torrent of
idolatry, and be so much better than my fathers, as to
destroy the evil which they left unchecked in the
land. But I have failed, and am no better than
they. Take away my life now." But had he only
known human nature better, this dying-down of
enthusiasm on the part of the people would not have
surprised him ; for nothing is more hollow and fluctuating than popular applause. He forgot that the
system which he was opposing had human nature,
worldly interest, and earthly fashion on its side, and
that it was too deeply rooted to be overturned by a
" huzza." Grand as the Carmel triumph had been,
that was not the winning of the campaign : it was
rather but the sounding of the advance, or, at best,
the achievement of the first victory. The iniquity
which he wished to remove was not to be destroyed
in a day. It needed that the principles which he
had announced, and the proofs which he had given
on the mountain, should be received into men's
minds, talked over in their homes, and prayed over
in their closets, before any general effect could be
produced ; and for all these things time was required.
Nay, it might even be that his own martyrdom by

Jezebel might have contributed as much to the reformation as the scene on Carmel; even as the smoke of Patrick Hamilton's burning at the stake was said to have infected all on whom it blew, and so to have commenced the Scottish Reformation. In any case, it seems to me that there was impatience, natural indeed, yet in its essence unbelieving, manifested by Elijah. He was looking for the harvest while yet the seed had but just left his hand, whereas "the husbandman waiteth for the precious fruit of the earth, and hath long patience for it, till he receive the early and the latter rain." Let us learn a lesson here also.

Let us not be unduly elated by momentary success. It is pleasing at the moment, but it may not last, and we must discount a great deal from it when we come to call for self-denying efforts for the Lord's cause. Not every one who cheers on Carmel will rally round us at Jezreel, with Jezebel denouncing death upon our head. There is much truth in the words of Robertson here, though they be tinged a little by the bitterness of his own experience : "What is ministerial success? Crowded churches, full aisles, attentive congregations, the approval of the religious world, much impression produced? Elijah thought so ; and when he discovered his mistake, and found out that the Carmel applause subsided into hideous stillness, his heart well-nigh broke with disappointment. Ministerial success lies in altered lives and obedient, humble hearts, unseen worth recognised in the Judgment-day." [1]

---

[1] "Sermons," Second Series, p. 105.

Let us beware, again, of falling into undue depression when the favour of the multitude dies down.
It is not right to take that as a gauge of our real
success or failure. There are some things to the
merchant better than a fortune; there are some things
to the minister more truly success than overflowing
audiences. His grandest success will not be in
immediate "hosannas," but rather in the gradual
effects of his teaching and his example, through a
course of years, upon those to whom he ministers.
The tear-drop glistening in the eye of one penitent,
brought to Jesus' feet by his tender words; the knowledge that some poor victim of evil habit has broken
asunder his chains under his influence; the perception
of growth in steadfast holiness of character in many
of his flock—these, to him, ought to outweigh a thou-
sand-fold the compliments of the crowd and the
applause of thronging multitudes; and in the days
when he finds himself deserted, his truest solace
will be the remembrance that the truths which he
has taught have taken living root in many hearts,
and are bringing forth fruit to the honour of his
Master.

Let us be sure, therefore, that we put a right value
upon that which we have before we hanker after that
which we have not; and, above all, let us be
moderate in our expectations. Luther had to say to
Melancthon once, when that great scholar was under
the juniper-tree, that "old Adam was too strong for
young Philip;" and many an earnest worker would be
spared much distress, and be prevented from running
away from his post in despair, if he were more correctly to appreciate the difficulties which he has to

encounter, and more wisely to estimate the character of those results for which he is to look.

Finally, here, we may perhaps see another cause of Elijah's depression in the fact that he was giving too great prominence to himself in the matter. On a memorable occasion in Samuel's life, when he was greatly distressed at the thought that the tribes would not longer have him as their judge, but desired a king, the Lord at once rebuked and strengthened him by saying, " They have not rejected thee ; but they have rejected Me." So, when Jonah lay in anger under the gourd, the great cause of his misery was, that he was thinking more of his reputation as a prophet than of Jehovah's glory in the salvation of the Ninevites. In like manner, I think I can trace in Elijah's somewhat self-complacent rehearsal of his doings, when God questioned him in Horeb, that he was suffering in some degree from wounded self-conceit.

It is remarkable that those who are the loudest in their complaints of want of success are often, also, those who have the highest idea of their own powers. By a singular law of compensation, they make up for the lack of appreciation of them by others by an undue opinion of themselves. I am very far indeed from saying that Elijah belonged to that class; yet I cannot but feel that, in this one instance, he was the victim of wounded pride. So just to let him see what he would be, or, rather, what he was when left to himself, God let him alone ; and he ran away.

Let us learn from all this to think more of God's glory than our own reputation. The cause is of infinitely more importance than any individual among us. When we begin to fret over our own lack of

recognition, we are in danger of falling into some
disgrace, and, by and by, may find ourselves under
the juniper-tree in the saddest and darkest despair,
crying, " I am aweary, aweary ; I would that I were
dead ! " The humble man is ever the most patient,
and the most persistent in the service of the Lord.

But now let us follow the history, and note how
Jehovah dealt with His servant in his circumstances
of depression. And here you will observe, first, that
He gave him rest and refreshment. He let him lie
still and sleep, that by the restoring influence of
slumber his frame might recover its elasticity. He
did not awake him by violence ; but when the time
came that he should eat, He sent His angel to prepare
nourishing food for him, and gently to invite him to
partake of it. A second time this was done for him,
and he was admonished to eat heartily, because a long
journey was before him. Who can read this story
without being reminded of our Lord's treatment of
the multitude when it was said that " He would not
send them away fasting, lest they should faint by the
way " ? Then, whether by divine direction or of his
own motive we cannot tell, he arose and went to
Horeb, that amidst those bare and lonely peaks,
where Jehovah gave the law to Moses, he, too, might
meet his covenant God.

Now, what considerate kindness have we in all this !
Of a truth God " will not break the bruised reed, nor
quench the smoking flax." His servant had erred,
yet he was just then in no proper state to be admonished for his error ; so God strengthened him, in order
that he might bear reproof. As when a father has
gone in search of a runaway son, and finds him stricken

down with a dangerous fever, he sits down and nurses him with tenderness, saying no word of blame until he has been in some measure restored to health, so the Lord here will not put too heavy a load upon the heart-broken prophet, but makes the most appropriate provision for his comfort and support. Behold the gentleness of our God ; and whensoever we are lying under the juniper-tree, let us recall with re-assurance this kindness shown to Elijah, and rest in the conviction that in some similar though non-miraculous way He will visit and sustain us.

But not less remarkable is the admonition, partly in words and partly in supernatural symbol, which the Lord addresses to His servant ; nor can we read the account of it without having recalled to us a similar revelation made by Jehovah to Moses in the same locality. Both were immediately consequent upon a signal execution of righteous judgment. Moses had come from the slaying of the idolaters ; Elijah from the destruction of Baal's priests. In both there was a clear and particular reference to the mercy and graciousness of God ; but the one was given to strengthen a faithful servant, the other to correct the false impressions of a sincere though erring prophet. To Moses the Lord said, " My presence shall go with thee, and I will give thee rest ;" to Elijah he said, " What doest thou here ? " The question was emphatic, and must have suggested far more than it expressed. Thou, my appointed messenger and chosen champion, here ! so far from the scene of thy labours and the post of duty ! So He probed the conscience of Elijah ; and so, not in the desert of Sinai, but in the highways of business, or in the by-

ways of sin, or in the solemn assembly, He often
probes ours.

Ah, how frequently have we heard, sounding in our
secret ears, these same words of searching inquiry,
What doest thou, a professed adherent of the Lord
Jesus, here, in the gambling-room, or haunt of
sensuality or intemperance? What doest thou, a real
disciple of the Lord, here, among those who make a
mock at His name and a jest of His religion? What
doest thou, a selfish, godless man, here, at the table
of the Lord, with those who truly love and serve Him?
Friends, when this stern voice is heard by us thus, let
us welcome it as the utterance of God, and resolve
that by His help it shall never again require to be addressed to us. " Faithful are the wounds of a friend,
but the kisses of an enemy are deceitful."

Then, after Elijah had attempted to vindicate himself, in words that seem to reveal the wounded self-
love to which I have referred, saying, " I have been
very jealous for the Lord God of hosts: for the
children of Israel have forsaken Thy covenant, thrown
down Thine altars, and slain Thy prophets with
the sword; and I, even I only, am left; and they
seek my life, to take it away." The Lord said: "Go
forth, and stand upon the mount before the Lord.
And, behold, the Lord passed by, and a great and
strong wind rent the mountains, and brake in pieces
the rocks before the Lord; but the Lord was not in
the wind: and after the wind an earthquake; but the
Lord was not in the earthquake: and after the earthquake a fire; but the Lord was not in the fire: and
after the fire a still small voice. And it was so, when
Elijah heard it, that he wrapped his face in his mantle,

and went out, and stood in the entering in of the cave. And, behold, there came a voice unto him, and said, What doest thou here, Elijah?" And this new inquiry he answered after the former manner.

Now, various interpretations of this spectacle have been suggested, but to my mind it seems to be a symbolical delineation to the prophet of the nature of the work which he had done, and a suggestion to him of that which had been wanting in order to the attain-ment of the success on which his heart had been set. There had been about him much of the whirlwind, the earthquake, and the fire. He had said and done much to terrify and alarm. But he was to learn that God was not in these things. These were but the awful outriders of His majesty; but that majesty itself is gentleness.

Here, therefore, as it appears to me, a great principle was unfolded to Elijah, and to all workers for God, and an intimation is given that, while they may need to use the earthquake and the fire, the secret of their power will ever be in "love." It was as if Jehovah had said, "But half of thy work is done, and that half the least profitable and powerful. Thou hast used the terror of the whirlwind. Go back, and try with men the still small voice of tender-ness and compassion." Not John the Baptist, but Jesus, is the regenerator of men; and though John must go before Jesus, yet to expect that he shall succeed in reforming the world is as absurd as to suppose that the ploughshare and the harrow will produce a harvest without the genial heat of the sun and the kindly rain of the clouds.

Then, having given Elijah this lesson, the Lord

says to him, "Yet have I left me seven thousand in Israel, all the knees which have not bowed unto Baal, and every mouth which hath not kissed him." Things were not so bad as to the prophet's jaundiced eye they looked. However hardly we may judge of matters, they are usually better than we deem, and in any case we must not let ourselves complain of lack of success until we have patiently exhausted all inquiries, and can speak from fullest knowledge. Not in the shout of the multitude on Carmel, but in the existence of those hidden ones, must Elijah see the true results of his faithful labours.

One thing, however, needs to be said here : God does not excuse these seven thousand for their silence. They ought to have declared themselves ; and if they had done so, perhaps Elijah's flight had never occurred. Ah ! how many servants of God have pined in melancholy, because none of those whom they have been the means of benefiting ever came to say to them, " God bless you, you have done me good."

When Chalmers was in the very zenith of his popularity in Glasgow, and crowds were gathering every Sabbath round his pulpit, he was walking home one evening with a friend, who told him of a soul who had been converted through the instrumentality of a sermon which he had preached. Immediately the tear-drop glittered in the good man's eye, and his voice faltered as he said, "That is the best news I have heard for long. I was beginning to think that I had mistaken the leadings of Providence in coming to your city ; but this will keep me up." And how many similar cases might be told ? Grumblers come often enough to the pastor, complaining that they have been neglected, or that things are not just as they want them to be ; but the people who are really upheld and comforted and blessed keep themselves hidden, until, too often, with his energies broken and his spirit crushed, the minister gives up in despair. Many an Elijah who has fled to the wilderness might have kept his post, if only those whom he had strengthened by his labours had come to him and encouraged him by their affection.

Finally, observe that God gives the prophet here some new work to do. He will take him out of himself by sending him on a new commission : " Go, return on thy way to the wilderness of Damascus : and when thou comest, anoint Hazael to be king over Syria ; and Jehu the son of Nimshi shalt thou anoint to be king over Israel : and Elisha the son of Shaphat of Abel-meholah shalt thou anoint to be prophet in thy room." There are few ministries more healing than that of work. A friend of mine in the pastorate, who had lost his wife, once said to me that he had no true comfort till he resumed his work. Kind counsellors had sent him to one place and another, assuring him that change of scene would do him good ; but his first consolation came to him through his ministry for others. And so it will be with us. The standing pool breeds fetid weeds and harbours croaking frogs; the running stream filters as it flows, and sings the while a happy song in the Creator's ear. Let us seek to keep our happiness in keeping at our work, for by the Gospel of Jesus labour has been transfigured into a means of grace.

Thus have I sought to bring before you the practical instruction of this chapter. Despondency may be on us now, or it may come to us in the future ; but in either case, let us remember God's dealings with Elijah, and so the lesson of this evening will be like God's own hand held down to us, by grasping which we may lift ourselves up from our dejection, and sing, " Why art thou cast down, O my soul ? Hope in God, for thou shalt yet praise Him, who is the health of thy countenance, and thy God."

IX.

ABEL-MEHOLAH.

A T the close of the last act of the stirring life-drama
of Elijah, the curtain fell before the desert-cave
of Horeb, where, after the passing-by of whirlwind
and earthquake and fire, we heard the still small
voice, followed by the Divine reproof and admonition ; and now, by one of those rapid transitions for
which this prophet's history is remarkable, the scene
is changed, and we look upon " the laughing brightness of a river-bordered meadow," with happy
ploughmen following their steers, and preparing the
furrows for the precious seed. The place is Abel-
meholah, literally, " The meadow of the dance ; "
therefore, as we may believe, the chosen resort of
the youth of the surrounding districts in all their
times of rural festival. It was situated in the plain
of Jordan, about ten miles south of Beth-shean, and
between that and Shechem. Long ago it had been
the refuge of the host of the Midianites when they
were pursued by Gideon ;[1] but now it is in the possession of Shaphat, who, eager to take advantage of

[1] Judges vii. 22.

the favourable change which the late rains have
brought, has sent all his labourers into the field to
plough.

It is a busy scene, for there are twelve ploughs at
work, each drawn by a yoke of oxen ; and with the
last of the twelve, bringing up the rear and superintending the movements of all the rest, is the beloved
son of the farmer, who thinks it not beneath him to
engage in manual labour.   But though we are all
familiar with such agricultural operations in our own
country, there are some things in the spectacle before us which are quite peculiar, and which call for
explanation.   The first is the shape and character
of the ploughs employed.   They are, indeed, of the
rudest description, and as far as possible from
equalling the elaborate implements which among
us is so denominated.   They are each, in fact, little
else than a stout branch of a tree, from which pro-
jects another limb, shortened and pointed ; and they
are so light that a man may easily carry his own,
and may guide it with one of his hands.   You
observe, too, that the different ploughmen are not
spread over the meadow, each working at a separate
portion of it, as would be the case with us ; but they
are following each other in line, and going over and
over again the same furrow, Elisha having the last
yoke, as the place of honour.   This is owing to the
fact that the ploughs are so insignificant and slight
that they merely scratch the soil.   Hence any
number of them may follow one another, each doing
its own little share in turning up the earth ; and
even after they have all passed over it, the furrow
will not be deep, so that they may have sometimes

to return along the same line, and thus go back and forth until the work has been satisfactorily accomplished.

Ploughing thus at Abel-meholah is a social thing. The men can talk and joke and laugh as easily as upon the harvest-field, and therefore you need not be astonished at the mirthful sounds that meet your ear as you look down upon the happy company. It is no place this for private meditation ; and yet as we shall see, a holy heart may serve God as really and as acceptably amidst the labour and the frolic of this busy meadow as does the high-priest within the courts of the Temple at the hour of evening sacrifice. Ay, and yonder comes the token that this service is a sweet savour to the Lord. For, lo ! on his way from Horeb to Damascus, his face yet saddened by the sorrow which his flight has caused, and his gait a little less defiant than before, as if yet he scarcely felt restored to himself, Elijah steps all unheralded upon the field; and plucking his mantle from his shoulders, he throws it over Elisha. That is all. He stays not to utter a word, but passes on as if there were something in the future beckoning him forward, and forbidding all delay.

It seems a strange proceeding ; and, to our Western eyes, it looks as if the stern old prophet had so far relaxed as to indulge in some practical jest at the young farmer's expense. But no, it cannot be a joke ; for he who is most intimately concerned, leaving his plough midway in the furrow, runs after the Tishbite, and meekly asks if he may go back and gave a farewell kiss to his parents ere he leave them. To this Elijah answers, " Go back again, for

what have I done to thee?" That is, not as the
cursory reader is apt to imagine, "Go back, for I
have done nothing to thee," but rather, "Return;
see that you remain not with them, or delay beside
them, for you know full well the solemn significance
of that which I have done." And what was that
significance? Elisha, as we must suppose, was well
acquainted with the appearance and office of Elijah.
He knew him to be the prophet of the Lord; perhaps, also, he had heard, or, as one of the vast
assemblage on the plain beneath the brow of Carmel
he had seen, what the Tishbite had done in honour
of Jehovah; and the casting of this robe on him he
knew to be the designation of himself as his coadjutor and successor in the holy office.

Dr. Jamieson, in his "Eastern Manners," has given
a full explanation of this symbolic act. He says:
"This ceremony has always been considered by
Eastern people an indispensable part of the consecra-
tion to the sacred office. It is in this way that the
Brahmans are still invested with the priestly character, a yellow mantle being thrown across their
shoulders, which is buckled round the waist with a
sacred ribbon; and it is in this way, too, that the
Persian Sufis are appointed. The master, in anticipation of death, selecting one of his favourite pupils,
bequeaths his antiquated garment to the youth, who
by that act is publicly recognised as his successor,
and looked upon as inheriting along with the mantle
the virtues and powers of his venerable precursor.
It was evidently owing to the prevalence of the same
Asiatic sentiments among the Israelites that the
succession to the prophetic office was determined by

the descent of his master's cloak upon Elisha; and so well was the action understood, as conveying to the servant the spirit and authority of the master, that he was universally acknowledged as the successor of that eminent prophet, and the leading champion in his age of the cause of God."

It was, therefore, because Elisha knew the meaning of Elijah's act, and because he heard in it the voice of God calling him to leave his father and mother, and give himself entirely up to the work of Jehovah among his countrymen, that he ran after Elijah and made the request he did. He saw that, if he obeyed that call, he must forsake his home and kindred, and he wished for an opportunity to say one formal and affectionate farewell. Henceforth he was to put his hand to another plough; and that he might not be tempted to look back after he had begun his new occupation, he wishes now to go and say good-bye to his parents and his friends. It was not, therefore, because he wanted to excuse himself for not obeying the call, but rather because he desired with his whole heart to obey it, that he asked permission to return; and so we account for the difference between the answer which Elijah gave to him, and that which Jesus gave to the man who presented a similar request to him.[1] The man who said to the Lord, "I will follow Thee; but let me first go bid them farewell which are at home at my house," was a waverer; he was trembling on the verge of decision, and was, by reason of the strength of his family affection, in danger of deciding wrong. Hence Jesus said to

---

[1] Luke ix. 61, 62.

him, in language probably suggested by this very
incident, "No man, having put his hand to the plough,
and looking back, is fit for the kingdom of God."
Elisha, however, was already determined to obey the
call, and so he readily obtained the permission which
he sought.

But surely this is a strange way to say farewell.
Here are no tokens of regret.   No tears are shed on
either side ; or if they are, they are tears as much of
joy as of sorrow, for Elisha is stepping upward to a
loftier sphere than that which heretofore he has filled.
Hence he gives an extemporised banquet to his
family and companions. He parts from them with
gladness, not, indeed, because he is leaving them,
but because he is going to a nobler work, in the call
to which he sees the highest honour of his life.   Like
as when Matthew left his toll-booth to follow Christ,
he gave a great feast to his companions, so Elisha
here makes a festival for his associates ; then, hurry-
ing from the joyous board, he hastens after Elijah ;
and as the curtain drops again, we see the ploughmen
in the field, but Elisha is not there ; for he has gone
to work in the greater field of God's own Church, and
henceforth he is to deal with human hearts, and to
scatter in them the seeds of God's eternal truth.

There is much in this history to give us encouragement and direction.   Let us linger awhile to gather
up its lessons.

Observe, then, in the first place, the care exercised
by God in securing a constant succession of teachers
for His people.   He is always independent of any
individual man.   No one person is indispensable to
the carrying forward of His gracious designs ; for as

one after another disappears, it is invariably found that His forerunning care has anticipated the blank, and prepared already some other servant to step in and fill it up. When Aaron was sent up Mount Hor to die, he was commanded first to array his son Eleazar in the robes of the high-priesthood, and to anoint him to the office which he himself had held; and before Moses began the ascent of Pisgah, from whose summit he looked, for the first and last time, on the land of promise, he had charged Joshua in Jehovah's name to take his place. So, again, when David was prevented from fulfilling the cherished desire of his heart, and was not permitted to build the Temple for whose erection he had gathered so many materials, he was told that Solomon, his son, a man of peace, would enter upon and finish his beloved work. In like manner, in New Testament times, just as Stephen disappears from view, Saul, who was afterward called Paul, comes in sight, and takes up the particular department of work for the Christian Church which, in his address before the Council, the protomartyr had already made his own.

But so it always is; Jesus has declared that the gates of the grave shall not prevail against His Church; and just as, here, Elisha was ready to take Elijah's place, it will commonly be found that when one servant of the Master is removed from earth, or is sent to another field of labour, there has been, all unconsciously to himself perhaps, and to those around him, another led, through a course of training, to take the post which has been vacated.

The Church does not depend on any man, or any set of men; it rests on Christ; and from its ascended

Lord it receives, always according to its need, "some apostles, and some prophets, and some evangelists, and some pastors and teachers, for the work of the ministry, for the perfecting of the saints, for the edifying of the body of Christ."[1] Individuals die, but the race abides; believers die, but the Church remains; ministers are removed, but the ministry continues; for at the head of all is the Lord Jesus, and He "is the same yesterday, to-day, and for ever." To Him, therefore, let all application be made when churches need an under-shepherd. "He walketh among the candlesticks, and holdeth the stars in His right hand;" and if He send one servant to work elsewhere, be sure that He will find another to take up the labour which is left. Herein is that saying true, "One soweth, and another reapeth." The seed which has been scattered under one minister has not all sprung up, when another, sent by God, will come to quicken its growth, and to fill his bosom with the harvest sheaves; and there shall come a day—the crown of all our days—when the work of each shall be made apparent, and "he that soweth and he that reapeth may rejoice together."

Observe, in the second place, here, the honour which God puts upon industry in one's common daily work. Elisha was not called while he was engaged at his private devotions, though, judging of his character from the ready response which he made at this time, we are warranted in saying that his closet would not be neglected; but it was while he was following the plough that Elijah came upon him, and

[1] Ephesians iv. 11.

threw his mantle over him. God would thus teach us that we must not neglect our daily business, and that His rich blessing will descend upon us while we are serving Him, whether that service be of a specially devotional sort, or of a more common and ordinary description. He is pledged, indeed, to hear His people when they call upon Him ; but He has often, also, come to them while they were seeking to glorify Him by honest industry. Moses was keeping his father-in-law's flock when God appeared to him in the burning bush, and commissioned him to conduct the exodus of His people from the land of bondage. Gideon was found by the angel at his threshing-floor when he was made the leader of his people against their Midianite oppressors. David was sent for from following the sheep in the fields of Bethlehem to receive the anointing oil from Samuel's horn. Amos was taken from tending his herd at Tekoah when he was sent to Israel with a message from the Lord ; and in the early history of the Gospel, if Nathanael was called to follow Christ from his seclusion under the fig-tree, Peter and James and John were taken from the fisherman's boat, and Matthew from the tax-gatherer's office. God thus honours work, when work is done faithfully and for Him.

But some there are who think that this call is no honour. They imagine that to be a prophet, or teacher, or apostle, or a minister of Christ, is a smaller thing than to be a successful merchant or a great manufacturer; and so they deliberately refuse to obey the call. I willingly allow, indeed, that there are many in the ranks of the ministry who have imagined that they heard God's call, whereas they are signally unfitted for the office into which they have thrust themselves. But it is just as true that there are multitudes in business life who would have adorned the ministry, and who would have been eminently successful in it, but who, when they heard God calling them, deliberately preferred the gains of the world to the honour which He had designed for them.

It is the complaint of all our churches that our young men seem lacking now in that spirit of enthusiasm and self-sacrifice which would lead them to consecrate themselves to the service of God in the ministry of the Gospel; and it is feared that the prizes of commerce prove a stronger attraction than the happiness of winning souls. If this be so, let this worldly spirit in our youth be solemnly rebuked by the narrative that has been to-night before us. There is no higher honour God can put upon a man than to call him to the ministry of His Son; there is no greater joy the soul can know than that of leading another soul to Christ; and if the highest angel might choose, among all earthly occupations, that which he would most delight in, it would be to tell again to men, as of yore he told to the shepherds of Bethlehem, the glad tidings, "that unto them is born a Saviour who is Christ the Lord." All work is honourable; and the followers of Him who for many long years wrought as a common carpenter in Nazareth need never be ashamed of horny hands and hammering toil. Christ has consecrated and ennobled all such handicraft, and whoso sneers at that blasphemeth Him. But yet, of all labour which the earth can furnish, that is the most honourable which is put forth in the ministry of the Gospel; and he who, when the mantle of God's

call falleth over him, declines to wear it, is refusing
one of the noblest, happiest, most useful, and most
honourable positions which the Lord can give. When
God called Elisha, he said to him, "Come up higher."
"They that be wise shall shine as the brightness of
the firmament; and they that turn many to righteousness, as the stars for ever and ever."

Observe, in the third place, that special training is
needed for special work. We saw that for the stern
duties which Elijah had to discharge, he was particularly fitted by the solitude of his early life, and the
rugged grandeur of the scenes in the midst of which
he dwelt. Elisha, on the other hand, was trained for
the more peaceful and gentle ministry on which he
was sent, by the home-life of his father's house, and
the quiet influences of agricultural pursuits. Like
many another minister, his first college was his home;
and there, as we are warranted in believing, from the
readiness with which they gave him up to his new
work, his parents trained him in the nurture of the
Lord. Among the seven thousand who had not
bowed the knee to Baal, as we believe they were,
they would speak with him often and long of Jehovah,
and the wonders which He had wrought of old in His
people's behalf, thus all unconsciously preparing him
for the future which God had planned for him; and
when the call to the prophet's office did come, they
did not interpose, heaping difficulty upon difficulty,
and doing everything they could to bar the way, but
they generously gave him up, feeling that God had
put the highest possible honour upon their home-
training by crowning it with His approval. Time was
when the office of the ministry was thus regarded by

the fathers and mothers of our churches ; but now, alas ! they too are poisoned by the atmosphere of the world; and, to have a ministry revived in numbers and in power, we must have first a revival of the family life out of which the ministers of the past did spring. Give us back the godly households of the past, and we shall not lack a devoted ministry.

But this was not the whole of Elisha's training. For seven years after the incidents which we have been considering, he was the companion and friend of Elijah ; and so he was under the best of preparatory influences for his work. In like manner, it is highly requisite that those who, in our day, are to be the spiritual teachers of others should themselves be specially instructed. I know, indeed, that many have sneered at our colleges and theological seminaries, and have styled the men that issued from them *man-made ministers*, while they have pointed us to the first preachers of the Gospel who were unlearned and ignorant men. But they who reason thus forget that the first apostles had the privilege, for three years and a half, of receiving the instructions and taking on the impress of Him who was emphatically "the Great Teacher," and that, in addition to this advantage, they enjoyed the special gift of the Holy Spirit, "to bring all things to their remembrance, whatsoever Christ had said unto them." This was certainly a very special and peculiar training ; and so far from its being an argument for no training at all, the case of the apostles is one of the strongest that can be cited in favour of the best system of educating the ministers of the Gospel.

It has been alleged, again, that the secular studies

of our colleges have a tendency to deaden the piety
of those who prosecute them, so that they who have
entered our seminaries all aglow with zeal have often
left them cold and dead, and utterly unfit either to
interest or edify their hearers. But this need not be
the case if these studies be properly pursued and
rightly superintended ; and if the training of the
ministry is important at any time, it is specially so
now, when questions of criticism, science, and
philosophy are discussed by the propagandists of
infidelity, with the view of unsettling men's faith in
the Word of God. There will always be splendid
exceptions to every rule, and in every age you will
find some of the noblest ministers who have never
been in a college in their lives ; but their cases are
no rule for others, and they themselves, from their
own experience, will be the most earnest in enforcing
special preparation upon others ; so that our young
men who present themselves for the ministry need
not murmur if they find that, as in Elisha's case, they
have to reach the goal of their desire through a seven-
years' service at the side of some Elijah.

Observe, in the fourth place, that God finds use
for the distinct individualities of His servants. There
are " diversities of gifts, but the same spirit." All
God's ministers are not made after the same pattern.
There are individual features of character and
disposition, as distinctive of each as are the outlines
of the face of each. John is quite different from
Peter, and Paul is distinct from both. What a
contrast do we find between Elijah and Elisha ! It
is impossible to give it vividness without anticipating
many of the statements of the history ; but you know

enough of both already to be convinced that I am
speaking truly. Elijah began his ministry with the
announcement of a terrible calamity; Elisha signalised
the commencement of his public work by the per-
formance of a miracle of mercy. Elijah dwelt apart
in the desert, like John the Baptist; Elisha abode in
the cities, and mingled with men in their homes and
in the streets, like him who was a guest at the feast
of Cana, and taught in the streets of Capernaum.
Elijah dealt in denunciation, and called down fire
from heaven to devour his adversaries; Elisha's
might was in his gentleness, and he went everywhere
carrying a blessing. Elijah with the plough and harrow
tore up the soil; Elisha followed, casting in the seed;
or, to go back to the parabolic miracle which was last
Lord's-day before our thoughts, Elijah was the whirlwind, the earthquake, and the fire; Elisha was the
still small voice. Each came in his own order; each
was excellent for his own department. The one
could not do the other's work, and both together
were needed for the service of God. So it is yet.
There are diversities of aptitude and character among
the servants of God; but all who love Him are His
servants, and the qualities of each, however diverse
from those of the others, are made subvervient to the
purposes of Jehovah's grace. Each has his own
beauty and excellence. The rose is not he violet,
neither the daffodil the primrose; but God has made
them all, and has revealed His wisdom distinctively in
each. So in the members of His Church there is a
variety in unity, and the effect is to manifest more
wonderfully to men and angels His own "manifold
wisdom."

Once more: the conduct of Elisha here furnishes us with a beautiful example of the spirit and manner in which we should respond to the call of the Lord Jesus Christ. If we have rightly represented his views as to the meaning of the act performed by Elijah on him, Elisha must have fully counted the cost of the step which he was about to take in responding to Jehovah's call. He knew that he must leave his home. He knew, also, that with an Ahab on the throne, a Jezebel in the palace, and an idolatrous population scattered over the country, the duties of the prophetical office would be not only onerous, but dangerous. Yet he conferred not with flesh and blood, but promptly and decidedly arose and went after Elijah. Now, so it ought to be with us and Christ. He does not call every one of us now to the office of the ministry, indeed, neither does He require us to leave our father's house in every case; but every man who hears the Gospel is required to renounce himself and his sins, to take Jesus for his Lord, and to follow Him in the sense of imbibing His principles and imitating His example. No matter though it should entail pecuniary loss or personal danger; no matter though it should estrange us from the closest earthly relatives, and separate us from our most cherished friends; no matter though it should demand the sacrifice of pleasures dear to us as a right hand or a right eye; no matter though it should put us in peril of the prison or the scaffold, we are required to "follow Him." Here are the terms: "Whosoever will be my disciple, let him deny himself," *i.e.*, renounce himself, "and take up his cross daily and follow me." Once again, O sinner! Christ has come to you and made this solemn call. Let Him not cast His mantle over you in vain. Let no sin hold you back from His service. Let no shame repel you from His allegiance. Let no fear frighten you from the ranks of His followers. Rise and go with Him. The very obedience which you render to His call will be itself within you a richer feast than that which Elisha spread before his fellows when he left his home. Go after Him at once; but as you go, remember that you must trust in His strength, and not in your own. Be not heady and high-minded, like him who said, "Lord, I will go with Thee to prison and to judgment," and who, ere long, denied Him; be steady, be resolute, be humble, like him who went right forward into trial with these words upon his lips: "None of these things move me; neither count I my life dear unto myself, so that I might finish my course with joy, and the ministry which I have received of the Lord."

X.

NABOTH'S VINEYARD.

1 KINGS xxi.

THE scene is in the city of Jezreel, where Ahab has his ivory summer palace, and whither he has just come from Samaria to take possession of a vineyard which lay contiguous to his park, and which he meant to turn into a flower-garden. He is in his royal chariot, and behind him [1] are riding Jehu, the son of Nimshi, and his comrade and subordinate, Bidkar—men destined, in after-days, to be the executioners of Jehovah's righteous retribution on the house of Jezebel, but now high in the favour of the reigning monarch. He is pointing out to them with pride the beauty of the situation, dwelling especially on the rounded completeness which this new acquisition gives to his fair domain, and unfolding to them the plan after which he means to lay it out, when, with the lightning-like suddenness so characteristic of all his movements, Elijah, in his hairy garment and leathern girdle, starts up before him, and rolls out the thunder of a new and terrible denunciation: "Thus saith Jehovah: Hast thou killed? and also

---

[1] 2 Kings ix. 25.

taken possession ?   Thus saith Jehovah : In the place
where dogs licked the blood of Naboth, shall dogs
lick thy blood, even thine."

What means this dreadful interruption to Ahab's
tour of inspection and admiration ?   What has the
king done to provoke this fearful doom ?   To answer
these questions we must go back a little, and recount
the particulars recorded in the early part of the
chapter which constitutes our subject for this evening.
Years have passed since that memorable night when
Elijah, with his mantle girt about him, ran from Carmel
before the monarch to the gates of this very palace,
and they have not been either uneventful in themselves, or entirely discreditable to Ahab ; for twice, by
the assistance of Jehovah graciously rendered, and
gratefully received, he has overcome in battle his old
Syrian enemy, Benhadad.   But this great prosperity
only filled his heart with pride and covetousness, and
he desired to signalise his victories by making some
splendid additions to the park surrounding his ivory
palace at Jezreel.   As it happened, there was a vineyard, the situation of which was hard by his land.
Indeed, it probably abutted in upon his grounds,
making what he conceived to be an ugly angle in his
possessions.   What more natural, therefore, than
that he should wish to straighten his boundary? or
what apparently more honest than his offer to its
owner : " Give me thy vineyard, that I may have it
for a garden of herbs, because it is near unto my
house, and I will give thee for it a better vineyard
than it, or, if it seem good to thee, I will give thee
the worth of it in money."   Perfectly fair, and in
ordinary circumstances, or in another land, one would

have expected that Naboth, to whom the vineyard belonged, would have been glad of an opportunity of obliging his royal neighbour by complying with his request, But the tenure by which the Israelite held his land was peculiar ; and there was another party to all such transactions, of whom Ahab took no note. Throughout Judah and Israel, Jehovah was the real owner of the soil ; and every tribe received its territory and every family its inheritance by lot from Him, with this added condition, "The land shall not be sold for ever ; for the land is mine ;"[1] and again, "Every one of the children of Israel shall keep himself" (or, as in the margin, "cleave to") "the inheritance of the tribe of his fathers."[2] It is probable, indeed, that in such a time of wide-spread idolatry as that which Ahab had introduced, this land-ordinance had been too generally disregarded ; but Naboth "feared the Lord." Though he was Ahab's nearest neighbour at Jezreel, he was, as I think we are safe in concluding, one of those who refused at the king's command to bow the knee to Baal ; so now, with every disposition in the world to oblige the king, he felt that he must obey God rather than man, and therefore he declined to sell his property. Had he been in debt to clamorous creditors, he might have had some colourable pretext for accepting the monarch's offer, though even then a reversion of the property to his family at the year of Jubilee would have been insisted on. But he had not even this excuse to plead, and therefore, with leal-hearted loyalty to the covenant God of Israel, he made reply,

---

[1] Leviticus xxv. 23.   [2] Numbers xxxvi. 7.

"The Lord forbid it me that I should give the inherit-ance of my fathers unto thee."

This answer utterly disconcerted Ahab; so that, as on a former occasion[1] when he was reproved by a prophet for his leniency to Ben-hadad, he went to his house "heavy and displeased," or, as we should now say, stubborn and "in the sulks." Like a spoiled child, who has been so much accustomed to his own way in everything that he knows not how to bear refusal, and lies down sprawling on the floor in the impotence of rage and disappointment, the monarch was actually so much affected that he took to his bed, and refused his food, at the same time declining to see or converse with any of his courtiers. He evidently had no thought of forcing Naboth to yield to his desires, or of laying violent hands either upon himself or on his property. But Jezebel was not burdened with any such conscientious regard for the rights of others; and when she learned what the cause of her husband's moping was, she bitterly taunted him with his scrupulous timidity, and inti-mated that she would make short work with Naboth and his inheritance. "What," said she, "you the king of Israel! and allow yourself to be thus dis-obeyed and defied by a common yeoman! You have been altogether too courteous and considerate in the offer you have made him. I will give you his vineyard, and pay nothing for it either!"

So, taking the royal seal, she wrote letters to the elders of Jezreel, intimating that some dreadful sin had been committed in their city, for which it was

---

[1] 1 Kings xx. 46.

needful that a fast should be proclaimed, in order to avert the wrath of Heaven. At the same time she named Naboth as the special object of the king's displeasure, and commanded that two false witnesses should be obtained, who should declare that he had blasphemed God and the king, for which, as she well knew, the law condemned every convicted one to death. To this precious document she affixed the royal seal, and then transmitted it to Jezreel, and calmly waited the result.

Nor had she reckoned without her host in the matter; for the rulers of Jezreel, either in dread of offending one whose revenge they knew was terrible, or eager to do a service to one to whom in temporal matters they were so largely indebted, or moved with envy against Naboth, as one whose piety had been a standing protest against their own iniquity, carried out her instructions to the letter. They held their religious service; they went through the form of a trial; and then they took Naboth [1] and his sons to the common place of execution, and stoned them to death, leaving their bodies to be devoured by the wild dogs which prowled after nightfall in and around the city. Then they sent and told Jezebel that her orders had been obeyed.

She received the news with undisguised satisfaction. It was nothing to her that God's name had been profaned; that religion had been dishonoured; that justice had been outraged; or that innocent blood had been shed. She had obtained her object; for the property of those condemned to death for

---

[1] 2 Kings ix. 26.

blasphemy reverted to the crown ; and she hastened
to carry the good tidings to her husband. " Arise ;
take possession of the vineyard of Naboth, the
Jezreelite, which he refused to give thee for money :
for Naboth is not alive, but dead."

One might have thought that Ahab would have
expressed some condemnation of this awful conspiracy, culminating in such a tragic horror! But
no. Like many in modern times, though he was
restrained by his conscience from committing murder
himself, he had no scruple in availing himself of the
results of such a crime when perpetrated by another.
He flattered himself that though he had no hand in
Naboth's death, he might, as well as another, "receive the benefit of his dying." So, summoning
Jehu and Bidkar to accompany him, he drove down
from Samaria to Jezreel, and was with them in his
newly-obtained vineyard, when Elijah struck terror
into his heart by the words which we have already
quoted.

When he heard the Tishbite's withering denunciation, fear and trembling gat hold upon him. His
conscience, never fully asleep, woke into stinging
activity, and he cried out, in horror, " Hast thou
found me, O mine enemy?" To which Elijah
replied, with all his ancient valour, "I have found
thee : because thou hast sold thyself to work evil in
the sight of the Lord. Behold, I will bring evil
upon thee, and will take away thy posterity, and will
make thine house like the house of Jeroboam the
son of Nebat, and like the house of Baasha the son
of Ahijah, for the provocation wherewith thou hast
provoked me to anger, and made Israel to sin. . And

of Jezebel also spake the Lord, saying, The dogs shall eat Jezebel by the wall of Jezreel. Him that dieth of Ahab in the city the dogs shall eat ; and him that dieth in the field shall the fowls of the air eat." These words, not forgotten for nearly twenty years by Jehu, who merely overheard them,[1] sunk like lead into the heart of Ahab, and took from him all the joy of his new possession, so " that he rent his clothes, and put sackcloth upon his flesh, and fasted, and lay in sackcloth, and went softly." There was yet some sense of justice in him ; and these outward symbols of sorrow were not hypocritical. He did not feign the feelings of which they were the signs. He was humiliated. He was sad. If it had been to be done again, he would not have allowed Naboth to be put to death. For so much let us give him credit. But though his repentance was sincere, so far as it went, yet it did not go far enough. He feared the punishment of his sin more than he hated the sin itself. There was no word of restitution. There was no change in the general current of his life. Yet, to show His gentleness unto him, and to give him another opportunity of coming to his full self, by returning wholly to his God, Jehovah said unto his servant, " Seest thou how Ahab humbleth himself before me ? Because he humbleth himself before me, I will not bring the evil in his days : but in his son's days will I bring the evil upon his house."

And the evil did come ! Let us complete the record by noting how it came, and when. As to Ahab himself: entering into league with Jehoshaphat,

---

[1] 2 Kings ix. 25.

the king of Judah and father-in-law of his daughter, he met his old Syrian enemies at Ramoth-gilead, where, though he disguised himself, a random arrow mortally wounded him, so that his chariot was filled with blood. They took the body to Samaria. And one washed the chariot at the pool of Samaria, and the dogs licked up his blood.[1] As to Ahaziah, the son of Ahab, we shall come upon the record of his death in our next lecture.[2] As to Joram, the brother of Ahaziah, we read that Jehu, immediately after his anointing by Elisha, conspired against him, and went to Jezreel, where Joram lay sick of wounds which he had received in battle; that there, suspecting perhaps some evil, Joram rose and went out to meet Jehu in this very vineyard of Naboth, where Jehu slew him.[3] As to Jezebel, we learn[4] that, immediately after the slaughter of Joram, Jehu caused her to be thrown out of a window of her ivory palace, so that she died; and her body, being left neglected, was eaten up by dogs. As to the seventy sons of Ahab—we learn[5] that they, too, fell under Jehu's avenging and relentless sword; " for he slew all that remained of the house of Ahab, in Jezreel, and all his great men, and his kinsfolk, and his priests, until he left him none remaining." There was much of human passion and cruel policy in all this, for which Jehu himself, as a free agent, was condemned and punished; but yet in and through it all the Lord was carrying out His own retributive providence, that men might know that His justice

---

[1] 1 Kings xxii. 38.   [2] 2 Kings i.   [3] Ibid. ix. 14-27.
[4] Ibid. ix. 33.   [5] Ibid. x.

slumbereth not. The mill of God grinds slowly, but it grinds to powder; and though His judgments have leaden heels, they have iron hands.

There is much in this old chronicle of sin and doom which it may profit us to ponder. Let me try to bring out of it some present day lessons of warning and admonition.

We are reminded by the incidents which have been before us of the important principle that happiness consists not in having, but in being. Here was Ahab on the throne of Israel, with every comfort and luxury which wealth and rank could confer, yet hankering after more, and when that was denied him, filled with the bitterest mortification! The blessings which he already possessed were forgotten in the misery which was produced within him by the refusal of Naboth to let him have his vineyard. His disappointment over that one little thing cast a shadow on all the great mercies which he already enjoyed, and this little dead fly made the whole pot of his precious ointment unsavoury. Nor is this a solitary instance. See that haughty Persian in his splendid house! He has just come from the imperial palace where he has been banqueting with the king and queen; and in the pride of his heart he has called his wife and children round him, that he might recount to them the honours with which he had been loaded. He tells of his riches, and his promotion above all others at the court, and how the queen had allowed no one to come with the king unto her banquet but himself, and had given him a special invitation for the following day. Then, as he thinks of his emergence from the palace, and remembers that the stiff-backed Jewish porter at the gate refused to make obeisance to him as he passed, all the gladness vanishes from his countenance, and a scowl of unutterable hatred darkens on his features as he adds, "Yet all this availeth me nothing, so long as I see Mordecai sitting at the king's gate." How many even to-day are letting their lives be darkened because some Naboth denies them a vineyard, or some Mordecai will not salute them! They forget that, even if they had the things which they so long for, happiness would be as far from them as ever, and some new object would take the place of their old grievance. They do lack one thing. But that one thing is not external to them, but within them. They lack a new heart, and until they get that they can have no abiding satisfaction. "Whosoever drinketh of this water shall thirst again." [1] You may write these words over every fountain of external possession. No matter what a man has if he have not a happy and contented spirit, he will be craving for something else; and as soon as he gets that, it will lose its charm for him, so that he will sigh again for something more. But this thirst is not so much a disease in itself as it is the symptom of that inner fever which is consuming the soul. To gratify the thirst, therefore, will not at all touch the seat of the malady. The soul must have peace imparted to it; and then the thirst will subside. Now, it is just this that Christ promises to do for us and in us by His renewing Spirit. Hence He says, "Whosoever drinketh of the water that I shall give him, shall

---

[1] John iv. 13.

never thirst, but the water that I shall give him shall
be in him a well of water springing up unto everlasting life." [1] The renewed man shall have a fountain
of happiness within himself; and will not depend on
external circumstances or earthly possessions for his
joy. His Lord will be to him better than a thousand
vineyards; and the approbation of Christ will be of
more value to him than the obeisance of any Mordecai. Perhaps there is here to-night some melancholy one, whose spirit is soured by reason of some
worldly disappointment, or some lack of that appreciation to which he fancies he is fairly entitled. Let
me entreat him not to misunderstand his own case.
These feelings are but the cryings out of your heart
and flesh for the living God. They are the thirstings
of your soul for that which can be found alone in
Him. Turn, then, and seek your all from Him and
in Him. "Wherefore do ye spend money for that
which is not bread? and your labour for that which
satisfieth not? Hearken diligently unto Him, and
let your soul delight itself in fatness: incline your
ear and come unto Him; hear, and your soul shall
live."

But we are reminded here, also, of the evil of
unhallowed alliances. But for Jezebel, Ahab had
not subjected himself to this dreadful doom. In this
scene, more than in any other of their history, we see
the distinctive character of each. Ahab was ambi-
tious; he was brave; he had in him many elements
of nobleness, and was not the weakling that many
have portrayed him. Where his conscience was

[1] John iv. 14.

clean, too, he could be bold. But he was less daring
and decided in evil than Jezebel, just because he had
more conscience than she. This kept him both from
the full enjoyment of the world, and from the inven-
tion of such diabolic plans as that which Jezebel laid
on the present occasion. He was, indeed, bitterly
mortified by Naboth's refusal to grant his request;
but there is no evidence that he would ever have
thought of murdering Naboth to get his vineyard;
while his cry of anguish to Elijah, " Hast thou found
me, O mine enemy?" shows that his conscience was
quick to respond to the admonition of the prophet.
Now, if, at the moment of his disappointment, he
had been blessed with a godly wife, she would have
led him to think of the comforts which he already
possessed, and, far from setting herself to acquire for
him the object of his desire by unlawful means, she
would have urged him to seek his happiness in something nobler than the vineyard of his neighbour. As
it was, however, Jezebel added the guilt of conspiracy
and murder to that of covetousness; and so their
names have come down to us stained with the infamy
of a deed which has few parallels for cruel injustice
and cold-blooded malignity. When he wedded her,
he thought only of the glory of his Zidonian alliance,
and the strengthening of his hands against his Syrian
foes; but now she makes him participator in a crime
which drew down the curse of extermination on his
house, and poisoned the happiness of his remaining
years upon the earth. Thus the very means which
he used to secure the glory of his kingdom and the
permanence of his dynasty proved the ruin of both.

How often, alas! in humbler instances have similar

results followed a similar course ! Dazzled with the
glitter of a fortune, or the glare of an exalted position,
a young person enters into the sacred alliance of
matrimony with one who has no moral stability or
Christian excellence, and the issue is certain misery,
with the probable addition of crime and disaster.
For in such an intimate union there cannot but be
a constant influence exerted by the one upon the
other ; and if it should happen that the greater decision of character is with the less scrupulous of the
two, then both together shall descend to depths of
wickedness of which, at first, the more worthy had
not dreamed. For weal or for woe, for eternity as
well as for time, few things are more important in a
man's or woman's history than the matrimonial connection which may be made ; and yet with what
thoughtlessness and frivolity too often is that connection formed ! It is a thing for joking and buffoonery;
or, perhaps, a matter of worldly wisdom or conveni-
ence ; whereas it ought to be entered into " only in
the Lord." Let the young people before me prayerfully ponder this important lesson ; and let them
resolve that whensoever they take this solemn step,
it shall not be " lightly or unadvisedly," but " soberly,
discreetly, and in the fear of God."

We are reminded, thirdly, of the perversion which
an evil heart makes of religious knowledge. One
cannot read this narrative without observing how
minutely Jezebel was acquainted with the requirements of the Mosaic law. She knew that blasphemy
was punishable with death, and that only at the
mouth of two or three witnesses could any one be
condemned ; and so, while professing great abhor-

rence of the sin which she falsely imputed to Naboth, she used her knowledge of the Books of Moses for the purpose of putting a fair judicial face on her murderous deed. As in modern times we have seen men employ their knowledge of law in such a way as to outwit the law itself, so she complied with the outward forms of justice, that she might give a righteous colour to her unrighteous proceeding! And then, how sickening to think of her, a votary of Baal, proclaiming a fast because some one had blasphemed God! The Spaniards have a proverb somewhat to this effect, " When the serpent straightens himself, it is that he may go into his hole." So when the unscrupulous suddenly manifest some punctilious regard for legal forms or for religious observances, you may be sure that they are after mischief. Some of the blackest crimes that have ever been committed have been perpetrated through the forms of law, or under the colour of religion. Is it not true that " the heart is deceitful above all things and desperately wicked "? and are we not forcibly impressed with the fact that no one is so daringly defiant in wickedness as he who knows the truth and disregards it? Mere knowledge never yet saved any one from ruin; for if the heart be perverted, everything that enters the head is only made subservient to its iniquity. Your educated villains are all the more dangerous because of their education ; and among godless men they are the most to be dreaded who have an intelligent acquaintance with the Word of God. Let us not rest, therefore, in our knowledge of the contents of this book, as if that were all that is required; for, unless we believe its statements and obey its precepts, our acquaintance with them will only increase our wickedness and aggravate our guilt. The Bible believed will be to us the richest of blessings; but disbelieved and disregarded, it will become to us the blackest of curses. Take heed, therefore, lest it should be to you as a millstone round your neck to sink you to the lowest depths of perdition.

We are reminded, fourthly, of the price which we have to pay for sin. What weighty words are these of Elijah to Ahab, " Thou hast sold thyself to work evil in the sight of the Lord." They imply not only that Ahab had given himself entirely over to iniquity, but also that he had done so at the price of himself. The great German poet has elaborated this thought into that weird production wherein he represents his hero as selling his soul to the mocking Mephistopheles. And it were well that every evil-doer laid to heart the moral of his tragic tale. That which the sinner gives for his unhallowed pleasure or dishonest gain is himself. Consider it well. O drunkard! you thought that you paid for your dissipation when you laid out your money on the counter of Boniface; but, bad as that was, there is another and far longer reckoning behind. You sold your senses into inactivity; your intellect into stupidity; your conscience into insensibility; your character into weakness; your business into bankruptcy; nay, if you continue in your dreadful habit, you will sell your life on earth, and your everlasting salvation, too. The bill may be drawn at a long date; but it will come due, and when it comes, you will be held inexorably to your bond. All this is the price; and for what? oh, for what? For a temporary exhilaration, to be followed by a degradation to a level lower than that of the brutes that perish !

O sensualist ! when you left the haunt of wickedness, you fancied that you had done with cost ; but no ! You sold the purity of your nature, the honour of your manhood, the tenderness of your conscience, the health of your body, and the life of your soul. In one express word, you sold yourself, and that self, if you repent not, for eternity. All these were in the bond you sealed when you entered on your course of iniquity ; and if you persist in it, no Shylock will hold you with a more remorseless grasp than he to whom you have given it. Hear it, too, thou dishonest trader ! who thinkest to enrich thyself by preying upon others. In the cant phraseology of an unscrupulous age thou boastest that thou hast sold thy victims ; but thou hast only sold thyself. Only thyself ! Ah, but that is everything. Thou hast given thy character, thy reputation, thy time, thy talents, thy soul's salvation, all for a few glittering coins, which, after all, thou must leave behind thee when thy body dies ! And this thou callest a shrewd, sharp transaction ! Oh, how thou art outwitted by the cunning Mephistopheles, who laughs at thine undoing ! Go to, ye blinded dupes ! and seek to unlearn this false philosophy, this unequal barter, this suicidal folly. You are selling yourselves in the market of iniquity for the veriest trifles, even as the savage barters whole islands for a few glittering beads. If ye will make commerce of yourselves, then sit down first and count the cost, as you try to solve this infinitely momentous question, " What shall it profit a man if he shall gain the whole world, and lose his own soul? Or what shall a man give in exchange for his soul?"

We are reminded here, fifthly, of the curse which attends ill-gotten gains. Jezebel thought that by her cunning management she had obtained Naboth's vineyard for nothing; but it cost her very dear. It entailed upon her the loss of her husband and of her sons, and resulted ultimately in her own destruction. God is not indifferent to evil, though He do not interfere by miracle to prevent its commission. It might have seemed, indeed, that His moral government was a delusion when such a one as Naboth was permitted to be slain by the emissaries of Jezebel's malignity; and one can sympathise as he looks on such injustice with the complaint of Asaph: "Behold these are the ungodly who prosper in the world; they increase in riches. Verily I have cleansed my heart in vain, and washed my hands in innocency." But when we widen our range of observation, we discover that for all such dishonesty and oppression there is, even in this life, a terrible retribution. The gains of ungodliness are weighted with the curse of God; and, sooner or later, that will be made apparent. Let no one think that because this record is in the Bible, and the fearful doom upon Ahab and his house was pronounced by Elijah, therefore there must be a difference between it and any modern instance of deliberate wrong-doing and injustice. For the moral government of God to-day is administered on the same principles as those which we find underlying this narrative. True, the dishonest man now pursuing his purposes in secret may have no Elijah sent to him, with the special commission to declare to him the sort of punishment which shall overtake him; but Elijah's God is living yet, and one has only to open his eyes, and mark the progress of events from year to year, to be convinced that "sorrow tracketh wrong, as echo follows song—on, on, on." He who holds gain by injustice will, sooner or later, come to ruin; and, if no restitution is made, they who inherit from him his blood-stained gold will be made sharers of his calamity. Let a man rudely trample upon the weak, and take by violence that to which he has no right, and it will cost him much; for the judgment of God is already on the way to him, and though it tarry long, it will fall heavily when it comes. Let a nation covet its neighbour's territory, and by force or fraud annex it to its own, then, though no Elijah come specifically to denounce it, the issue must be disastrous, and may be fraught with evil to many generations. "Be sure your sin will find you out," said Moses, on a solemn day, to the two and a half tribes that remained on the other side of Jordan; and it seems to me that few truths need to be more faithfully proclaimed in the ears of this generation. They dwell with much unction on the love and tenderness of God; and if they but took in the whole truth, they could not dwell too much upon it; but they forget the judicial aspect of Jehovah's character, and the awfully terrible nature of some of His retributions. It is no kindness, however, to keep these things out of view. God's government is retributive, and the wrong-doer must one day confront the wrong that he has done; nay, must confront the avenging God, who comes to reckon with him for the wrong. He may meet Him in some desolating stroke of His provi-

dence ; but he must meet Him on His judgment-
throne ; and if the sight of the servant of Jehovah so
appalled Ahab that he cried out with trembling,
" Hast thou found me, O mine enemy?" need we
wonder if, as he gazes on the great white throne, he
is impelled to cry to the mountains and rocks, "Fall
on me, and hide me from the face of Him that sitteth
on the throne, and from the wrath of the Lamb, for
the great day of His wrath is come ; and who shall
be able to stand"?

Finally—for I may not conclude in this terrific
strain—we are reminded here of the tenderness of
God toward the penitent. Ahab was filled with bitter
regret at what had been done, and God, who will not
break the bruised reed nor quench the smoking flax,
said that the evil should not come in his day.

He thus gave him another opportunity of becoming
truly repentant. This, so far as appears from the
narrative, Ahab did not improve ; still, that God
should have given it to him is an encouragement to
the real penitent to come to Jehovah's feet ; while the
fact that he did not really and truly repent, after all,
is a warning to the trembling procrastinator that,
unless he avail himself of his present tenderness of
feeling, he may never attain salvation. If God were
so considerate of Ahab, the idolater, the murderer,
the thief, will he not regard thee, O thou tearful one !
who art bemoaning the number and aggravation of
thy sins? Go, then, to Him ; and let this be thine
encouragement : "Let the wicked forsake his way,
and the unrighteous man his thoughts : and let him
return unto the Lord, and He will have mercy upon
him ; and to our God, for He will abundantly pardon."

But go at once; for if, after all this feeling on Ahab's part, his repentance was yet only temporary, and he perished at last, how knowest thou that it may not be so with thee if thou delay? Felix trembled before Paul, as Ahab did here before Elijah; and yet he, too, went no further. Agrippa was almost persuaded; but the "almost" never became the "altogether." Let these beacons on the roaring reef of procrastination warn thee of thy danger. Let the feeling of this moment stiffen into the principle of thy life. Let thy repentance be no mere regret for sin, but a loving and immediate acceptance of the Lord Jesus Christ as the Saviour of thy soul and the Lord of thy life. "To-day, if thou wilt hear His voice, harden not thy heart."

XI.

FIRE FROM HEAVEN.

2 KINGS i.

BETWEEN Elijah's interview with Ahab in the vineyard of Naboth, and his intercepting of Ahaziah's messengers on their way to Ekron, a period of at least three or four years must have elapsed. During that interval several events of national importance occurred. In particular, Ahab, forming a league with Jehoshaphat, attacked the Syrians at Ramoth-gilead; but the result, as Micaiah had foretold, had been fraught with disaster ; for Ahab was slain, and the Syrians were left masters of the field.

The death of Ahab had been followed by the accession of his son Ahaziah, who had proved himself to be the inheritor of his father's character as well as of his position; for "he did evil in the sight of the Lord, and walked in the way of his father, and in the way of his mother, and in the way of Jeroboam the son of Nebat, who made Israel to sin; for he served Baal, and worshipped him, and provoked to anger the Lord God of Israel, according to all that his father had done."

He came to the kingdom when it was weakened, and the people were dispirited, by the recent Syrian

defeat; and the first thing he had to do was to encounter a rebellion of the Moabites, who took advantage of the national exhaustion, and broke away from
the bondage of tribute under which they had been
held by Omri and Ahab. Under the brief reign of
Ahaziah, they were not able completely to regain
their independence, but they thoroughly effected their
emancipation in the days of Jehoram, his brother and
successor, as described at length in the third chapter
of 2nd Kings. Very recently an interesting light has
been thrown on this chapter of ancient history by the
discovery of the Moabite Stone, which was found by
the Rev. F. A. Klein, in 1868, at the entrance to the
ruined city of Dibon, and which was a monumental
record of the successful rebellion of Mesha, king of
Moab against the king of Israel after a forty years'
oppression by the house of Omri.

In neither of these times of war, however, does
Elijah come into prominence. His mission had not
to do so much with the relation of Israel to the surrounding nations as with the reformation of the tribes
themselves. The department of work which had
been committed to him was religious rather than
political. He was more concerned for the character
of the people than for the extent of the nation's territory or the amount of tribute paid by its depen-
dencies. Hence all his appearances had for their
object the destruction of some prevailing iniquity,
like the worship of Baal; or the denunciation of
some flagrant wrong, like the robbery and murder of
Naboth. There were other prophets in the land who
took note of the doings of the king or of the people
in their conflicts with other nations. Thus, when

Ahab let Ben-hadad slip out of his hands, an unnamed messenger was sent to rebuke him ; and when, again, he was to be warned of his danger at Ramoth-gilead, Micaiah was commissioned for that special purpose. Nor is it without significance, as an incidental proof of the effect which Elijah's ministry had produced, that there were now in the land men of God who were willing to go to prison, or even to death, rather than prophesy lies in Jehovah's name. But still, when sin in high quarters was to be exposed, or sentence against evil executed, Elijah was the minister to whom such work was entrusted. Thus we account for his appearance on the occasion described in the chapter which now lies before us for exposition.

Ahaziah, while walking on the roof of his palace, leaned incautiously on the frail banister of wicker-work which formed its only protection on the inner side, and as that gave way under his weight, he was precipitated to the court beneath, and seriously injured. In his weakness and alarm, he sent some of his servants to Ekron, the most northern of the five Philistine towns, where Baal-zebub, the god of flies, was worshipped ; and where, in connection with that idol's temple, there was one of those oracles which, in response to the inquiries of liberal devotees, gave out "flattering ambiguities" that, from their double or doubtful meaning, could not be falsified by any event. This action of Ahaziah's was a contemptuous ignoring of the claims of Jehovah upon him, and an evidence that he had withdrawn conclusively from the service of him from whom, as the King of Israel, he derived his authority, and to whom the whole allegiance of his heart and life was due. But as, when Saul went to consult a familiar spirit, God sent Samuel himself to confront him, to the dismay both of the witch herself and of the abandoned monarch, so now again, when Ahaziah sends to Ekron, the Lord commissions Elijah to intercept his messengers, and to give them an answer to their inquiries, not in vague and oracular phraseology, but in words of un- mistakable meaning and tremendous force : " Is it not because there is not a God in Israel that ye go to inquire of Baal-zebub, the god of Ekron? Now, therefore, saith Jehovah, Thou shalt not come down from that bed on which thou art gone up, but shalt surely die." This message given, the prophet, with characteristic suddenness, disappeared ; and the ser- vants of the king, deeming their journey to Ekron now unnecessary, returned and reported the Tishbite's words to their master.

When he heard their account, accompanied with a description of the appearance of him who had so strangely intercepted him, the king knew at once that Elijah had been with them ; and his heart was filled with bitterest enmity and fiercest rage. One might have supposed that after he had learned on such authority that he was so soon to die, he would have begun " to set his house in order," and would have given some serious thought to the future life on which he was about to enter. But no ! His sole concern seems to have been to get Elijah into his power, that he might destroy him for what he deemed to be his impertinent interference with his messengers to Ekron. He fell into the mistake of supposing that he had to do with Elijah rather than with Elijah's

God, and flattered himself that if he could only silence the Tishbite he had no one else to fear. Therefore, instead of turning in penitence to Jehovah, he turns in fury against the prophet. As the heathen Xerxes is said to have scourged the Hellespont, because its waves, in the violence of a storm, swept away his bridge, forgetting that he had to do with Him whom the winds and the sea obey; so Ahaziah took no note of Jehovah, whose servant Elijah was. The matter seemed to him to be only between him and the Tishbite, and not at all between him and the omnipotent God. And yet the means which he took for the apprehension of Elijah indicate that he feared him more than he did an ordinary man; for he sent a company of fifty soldiers, with their captain, to take him. We are not a little surprised at this, for, as Bishop Hall has pithily remarked, "If he had not thought Elijah more than a man, what needed a band of fifty men to apprehend him? and if he did think him such, why would he send to apprehend him by fifty?"[1] The probability is, however, that he looked upon the prophet as belonging to the class of wizards, or magicians, who had hidden resources of power which rendered them dangerous to single adversaries, and so he took this plan of overmastering him by a formidable array of numbers. But if this were so, he had miserably miscalculated; for when the military company were ascending the hill at the top of which Elijah had his retreat, and the captain called jeeringly to him, " Thou man of God, the king hath said, Come down !" he made reply, " If I be a man of

---

[1] "Contemplations," as before, p. 304.

God, then let fire come down from heaven, and consume thee and thy fifty ;" and forthwith they were
destroyed by the flaming bolt of the divine vengeance. No one of them survived to tell what had
happened to the rest; but, somehow, either by report
spreading out from the immediate neighbourhood,
or by the result of inquiries which he himself had
caused to be made, the king learned what had
happened ; and, instead of humbling himself at this
new manifestation of the power of God, he sent
another company of fifty with another captain, who
were also consumed in like manner. Undeterred
even by this repetition of the disaster, he sent a third
company with a third captain. But this time the
messengers were not in sympathy with their message ;
for, instead of approaching with a contemptuous
sneer and cynical defiance, as the others had done,
this officer and his men drew near with reverence.
When they called Elijah a man of God, they recognised the dignity that belonged to his office, and the
protection that encircled it ; and their leader made
this humble request : " O man of God, I pray thee,
let my life, and the life of these fifty, thy servants, be
precious in thy sight. Behold, there came fire down
from heaven, and burnt up the two captains of the
former fifties : therefore let my life now be precious
in thy sight." This was a different spirit from that
which the former companies had manifested ; so at
the suggestion of the Angel of the Covenant, who had
been mysteriously present with him as his guardian
all the while, the prophet went with the soldiers to
the palace, and was ushered into the bed-chamber of
the king.

But the presence of monarchy did not in any way discompose Elijah, or cause him to abate one iota of the message which he had already delivered to his servants. It was a singular occasion, and the whole scene stands out before the eye of the imagination with weird and wonderful distinctness. There lies the wounded monarch, writhing in his pain, and cowering before the fiery glance of the stern Tishbite's eye. He could send his soldiers to take him prisoner, but he could not meet that gaze. Around him are his courtiers and his counsellors, all amazed at the undaunted courage of the unarmed prophet, who comes to introduce into that presence the grim enemy who is not only the king of terrors, but also the terror of kings. He has no word of counsel ; no message of consolation ; no prophecy of deliverance. He stands, like Daniel, reading off from the wall the dread handwriting of remorseless doom : " Thou shalt not come down from off that bed on which thou art gone up, but shalt surely die ; " and then, ere yet any one has recovered from the startled awe which his words produced, he passes out from the palace, never again to be seen within its portals. Nor was his denunciation vain ; for it came to pass as he had said, and Ahaziah died, the second of that long list of victims who fell before the march of God's justice in its course of retribution for Jezebel's murder and robbery of Naboth.

This portion of the sacred narrative, like those over which we have already passed, is rich in suggestive lessons which are full of living interest and present importance, and we shall do well to pause a while, and gather them up for our warning and instruction.

Observe, then, in the first place, that we do not escape from God by running away from Him. Ahaziah perhaps imagined that, by betaking himself to Baal-zebub, he was taking sure means to evade all danger from Jehovah. It was easy for him, comparatively speaking, to shut God out of his heart, and to cut himself off from the number of those who professed to believe in Him, and render Him obedience; but he could not thus put himself beyond the pale of God's government, or place himself outside of the sphere of God's providence. If he will send his messengers to Ekron, the Lord has His Elijah ready to confront them with his sentence of doom. The sinner cannot get anywhere away from God. This is as true to-day as it was in the times to which this history refers. Men may repudiate all faith in these sacred books; they may defy natural laws; they may worship philosophy or science; they may even adopt the dark negation of the atheist's creed; but they cannot, after all, eliminate themselves from the domain of His government, or the circle of His providence. True, He has no miraculously commissioned prophet now to intercept them in their foolish attempts, as the stern Tishbite turned back the servants of Ahaziah; but He confronts them still in ways at once numerous and striking. There is conscience, that Elijah in the breast, to whose voice of expostulation and reproof He gives point and power. There is temporal calamity, with its lesson of arrest, as it brings men up, and makes them think of something mightier than mere natural law or human skill. There is family bereavement, as it turns them back from all their cherished purposes and cunning schemes, and bids them forecast the future of this earthly life. There is personal affliction, as it lays its subduing hand upon them, and makes them pause midway in their earthly pursuits, and compels them to reflect upon the time when they shall be taken away from everything that interests and occupies their minds in this present state of being. There is death, that mysterious visitant that comes ever unbidden, and tears them away from all their occupations, no matter how unfinished they may be, or how much they may desire to continue at them. These are God's Elijahs now, coming often upon men with the lightning swiftness that characterised the Tishbite's appearances, and thundering in their ears words of doom as awful as those which the prophet hurled at the heads of Ahab and his son. No captain and his fifty can apprehend these agents of God's government and providence. No money can bribe them into harmlessness; no power can bind them into impotence; no eminence can overawe them into subjection. The sinner can find no place on this wide earth where he will be exempt from their intrusion. Go where he will, he cannot go where God is not. He may shut his eyes to the truth of His existence; but he cannot thereby secure himself from the visit of His messengers. He may occupy his thoughts with other subjects, but he does not thereby deliver himself from liability to the afflictive dispensations of His providence.

These things come upon the believer as on other men. The only difference is that the believer, when they come to him, sees in them, not the messengers of judgment, but the ministers of grace; and is supported under them by the strength of unfaltering trust in Him who has declared that "all things work together for good to them who love Him who are the called according to His purpose." To the child of God these dispensations come as Elijah did to the widow of Zarephath, and they end in making him praise anew the mercy which kept the handful of meal from wasting, and the cruse of oil from failing. To the ungodly they come as Elijah did to Ahab, when, in the vineyard of Naboth, the king cried out, "Hast thou found me, O mine enemy?" But to both, these Tishbites come sooner or later. Behold, then, how foolish the unbeliever is! He does not, he cannot, get rid of trouble. The utmost he accomplishes is to deprive himself of that Divine alchemy within the soul which changes trial into blessing. He has the ache of conscience, but he will not accept that Saviour who alone can remove that stinging pain. He has the endurance of temporal calamity, but he will have none of Him who, in time of money panic and bankruptcy, can sustain him with the assurance of His support. He has the bitterness of bereavement, but he will not accept the tender ministrations of that Divine Redeemer who says, "Weep not. I am the resurrection and the life." He has to taste of death, but he shuts his soul against the entrance of Him who alone can enable him to say, "O death, where is thy sting? O grave, where is thy victory?" What, then, is the gain of running away from God? Gain? ah! it is tremendous loss. Oh ye, who are worshipping at the shrines of the world's Baal-zebubs, bethink ye what ye do when ye thus turn your backs upon Jehovah-Jesus; and let me to-night, in mercy to you, intercept you on the

way to Ekron. Is there no God here, that you
should seek to fill your souls with unsatisfying husks,
which can give you no delight? What will philosophy, or science, or wealth, or honour, or position
do for you in the day when these great agonies to
which I have referred are on you? Turn ye, turn ye,
from that cheerless path, and seek your life and joy
in Him who is the God and Father of our Lord Jesus
Christ.

Observe, in the second place, that terrible judgment is sure to overtake them that persistently and
defiantly reject the Lord. I refer here not so much
to the circumstances of Ahaziah's death (though,
taken in connection with Elijah's prediction to Ahab,
they, too, might illustrate my position) as to the
destruction by fire from heaven of the two captains
with their fifties. It has been supposed, indeed, that
the Saviour's reference to this portion of the Tishbite's
history, when, in answer to the question of James and
John as to the Samaritans, " Wilt thou that we command fire to come down from heaven and consume
them even as Elias did?" He said, " Ye know not
what manner of spirit ye are of;" and added, "The
Son of man is not come to destroy men's lives, but
to save them," [1] was a virtual condemnation of the
course pursued by the prophet. But this is an entire
mistake, and arises from a superficial perusal, both of
the history on which we have been commenting, and
of the words of the Lord which I have just quoted.
For, in the first place, though the fire came at the
word of the prophet, it was Jehovah that sent it; and

---

[1] Luke ix. 52-56.

we cannot suppose that Jesus would brand anything which the Eternal Father did with His reprobation.

Further, the words, "Ye know not what spirit ye are of," are not a condemnation of Elijah, but a reproof addressed to His disciples. He did not mean to say that the Tishbite was actuated by an improper spirit; rather He wished the sons of Zebedee to understand that the disposition by which they were animated was very different from that which characterised the prophet. As if He had said : "You think that in making the proposal which you have just put before Me, you are acting in the spirit of Elijah, but in reality you are moved by a very different impulse. Elijah was very jealous for the Lord God of hosts. He lived and laboured to promote the honour of Jehovah, and it was solely on that ground that he called for the fire which came with its destructive stroke at his bidding; but you are only jealous for yourselves. It is wounded pride that is speaking now in you : it was righteous zeal for the glory of his Lord that flashed forth in the command of Elijah."

Others, however, while honestly believing that there is no condemnation of Elijah in the words of our Lord, have supposed that the whole difference between him and the apostles is to be accounted for from the fact that the prophet belonged to the sterner economy of the law, while they were under the milder system of the Gospel. And they base this opinion on the Saviour's words, " The Son of man is not come to destroy men's lives, but to save them." Now, though almost every commentator has taken this view, I confess that it does not commend itself to my judgment, inasmuch as I cannot see that God's deal-

ings with hardened and defiant sinners are anywise
different under the Gospel from that which they were
under the law. To them who receive it the Gospel
brings peace; but to those who, against light and
entreaty, persistently reject it, there is judgment. In
the one, the Gospel minister is to God a savour of
life unto life; in the other, a savour of death unto
death; and we cannot get rid of the fact that to
those who trample underfoot the Son of God, the
darkness of Calvary is a thousandfold more terrible
than were the thunders of Sinai. The Samaritans
who would not accept Jesus had only then for the
first time heard of Him; and their rejection of Him
was the result of ignorance. It was no time, therefore, to move for their destruction; but when the
Jews refused, with determined pertinacity, to accept
the Lord, and would have none of His salvation, what
happened to them? Read the prediction of our
Lord upon the Mount, then peruse the account of its
fulfilment in the destruction of Jerusalem, as that is
given by Josephus, and tell me if it is not vastly more
appalling in its aspect of judgment than the description given here of the striking-down of these two
captains and their fifties. Yet all that was under the
Gospel dispensation. Therefore the death of these
men is not to be explained merely by the fact that
they lived under the so-called stern economy of the
law.

The simple truth is, that they were hardened and
defiant in their rejection of Jehovah as the covenant
God of Israel. They knew better than to have
sneered at Elijah as they did. It was not so very
long since the day of the Carmel controversy, and

they could not have forgotten the issue of it, not only
as regards Elijah, but also as regards Jehovah. But,
like Ahaziah, they had steeled their souls against
conviction, and stiffened their hearts against submission, and so they were destroyed, not from any rage
in the prophet, but in righteous retribution for their
stubborn refusal to bow before Jehovah. But, my
hearers, the same law of God's government holds
under the Gospel ; and gracious though it be, if we
harden our hearts against its acceptance, the same
retribution, only in a more terrible because eternal
form, will come upon us. We may not be punished
by temporal judgments, as Israel was with drought
and famine ; but if we repent not, the result will come
in " everlasting destruction from the presence of the
Lord and from the glory of His power." Read the
parable of the pounds in the nineteenth chapter of
Luke's Gospel, and say what mean these words :
" But those mine enemies which would not that I
should reign over them, bring hither, and slay them
before me." Peruse the Epistle of Paul to the Thes-
salonians, and tell me what interpretation you can
put on such expressions as these : " The Lord Jesus
shall be revealed from heaven with His mighty angels,
in flaming fire, taking vengeance on them that know
not God, and obey not the gospel of the Lord Jesus
Christ." Yea, fathom for me, if you can, the significance of these words in the Book of Revelation, " The
wrath of the Lamb." Are not all these illustrations
of the same law of retribution which we have seen
to-night at work in the destruction of these soldiers ?
And do they not all alike declare that if we despise
the gracious privileges of our present time of proba-

tion, and refuse to accept of the salvation which comes through believing submission to Jehovah, we, too, shall be destroyed? I delight not to dwell on this awful theme ; but love to you, as well as faithfulness to my Master, demands that I set it fully before you, and beseech you prayerfully to ponder it.

Observe, in the third place, the mercy that is shown by Jehovah to those who penitently and sincerely seek it. The third captain and his fifty were spared. Why? Surely here we cannot say, because they were under the stern dispensation of the law ; and the right consideration of their case will, I think, demonstrate that I am correct in my explanation of the destruction of the others. They were spared, because, convinced that Elijah was really a man of God, and that Jehovah was the true God, they came acknowledging his authority and suing for mercy. Now, blessed be God's name, this law of His government holds still. If we come in penitence and faith to Him through Jesus Christ, we shall be saved. They that truly seek Him shall ever surely find Him. Hence if the fate of the former fifties be fraught with solemnest warning, the mercy shewn to this captain and his men is full of the richest encouragement, and bids us improve our opportunities of salvation by securing now forgiveness and renewal. No matter though we have held out against the Lord till the present moment, if now we come to Him in faith, " He will in nowise cast us out." Oh! the infinite grace of these precious words, " I will in nowise cast out." They mean, " I will receive ; I will retain ; I will eternally bless." My hearer, let their attraction draw you to a speedy acceptance of the grace they offer.

Observe, finally, the prophet in the chamber of the dying monarch ; and notice, by way of contrast, the blessedness of the Christian minister at the sinner's death-bed. Macduff and others have drawn a historical parallel between this visit of Elijah to Ahaziah, and that of the good Bishop Ken to the dying profligate, Charles II. of England, so graphically described in the pages of Macaulay ; but, after all, every Christian minister, though required faithfully to unfold the guilt and danger of the sinner, is commissioned to proclaim pardon to the penitent, even though he be standing on the very threshold of that world where probation is unknown and only retribution rendered. Elijah, however, does nothing but read out his sentence of doom. There is no urging to repentance, as in the case of Daniel's appeal to Nebuchadnezzar. The stern, unbending terror of the announcement of the monarch's death is unrelieved by a single qualification. God be thanked, it is different now with the minister of Christ. With the case of the thief on the cross before him, he feels himself warranted at every dying sinner's couch to preach Christ and His salvation. No matter how degraded the poor victim may be ; no matter how aggravated may have been his guilt, or how terrible his iniquity, "Jesus Christ is able to save unto the uttermost all that come unto God by Him ;" and while the day of grace lasts, and the day of life endures, it is the duty, as it is the privilege, of the minister to point the dying one to the Lamb of God that taketh away the sin of the world. I say not this to induce you to put off your penitence until your dying hour. I say it rather to magnify the riches of the grace of God ; and having done that, I turn to reason with you in this wise. You admit that faith in Jesus Christ, and the peace which flows therefrom, are desirable things to die with. Let me ask, is it any too soon to secure them now ? If they are so valuable for the experience of a death-bed, they cannot but be useful in the exigencies and emergencies of daily life. Besides, how know you that you shall have a death-bed at all? You see from Ahaziah's case how brittle is the thread of human life. Some frail breastwork of lattice may give way with you, and the issue may be, not a season of pain and weakness, followed, as in his case, by death, but death upon the spot. A thousand contingencies there are, the occurrence of any one of which would end your life and your probation in a moment. Is it safe, then, to trust to that which, after all, may never be yours ?

Moreover, though you may have a death-bed, it may be one of mental unconsciousness ; or, worse still, it may be one of spiritual insensibility ; and the repentance which you thought would come at your call may still be far away from you. I glory to preach the Gospel to a dying sinner ; but I would not have you trust to a death-bed. There is one case in the Scriptures of a soul saved just ere the twelfth hour struck ; *one*—that no one, even at that late season, may despair—but only one, that no man in health should presume on such a contingency for himself. To night, therefore, let those who are yet unconverted submit their hearts and lives to the Lord Jesus Christ, and then their experience will be blessed, and their deaths will be safe. Let your motto henceforth be, " My life for Christ—my life for Christ!" and then you will have no need to fear Death, come when he may.

> " It matters not at what hour o' th' day
> The Christian falls asleep.   Death can not come
> To him untimely who is fit to die.
> The less of this cold earth, the more of heaven
> The briefer life, the earlier immortality."

XII.

THE ASCENSION.

2 KINGS ii.

WE have a false idea of the work of Elijah if we suppose that it was restricted to such public appearances as that which he made on Carmel, or such denunciations of iniquity in high places as those which he uttered in the vineyard of Naboth and the palace of Samaria. In the history of a nation it has often been noted that the periods of its highest prosperity are those which furnish fewest materials for the public annalist; and similarly in the life of a minister of God, the years of his most potent influence and most enduring work are frequently those concerning which his biographer can find least to say.

Controversy, like war, is noisy and demonstrative, and forces itself on the attention of the chronicler; but growth is a thing of quietness, and is withal so gradually manifested that it eludes the observation of the historian. I say not this by way of undervaluing controversy, for it has its own place and importance; and he who shrinks from it when the honour of Christ's name or the purity of Christ's Church is concerned, is as much to be condemned as is the

man who is an ecclesiastical Ishmaelite, with his
hands against every one, and every one's hands
against him. After all, however, the benefit of controversy is only temporary. It is an exposure and
defeat of error for the time ; but unless it be followed
up by the adoption of some measures for the permanent conservation of the truth, the evil will come
back, and the whole battle will have to be fought
over again. Therefore, though less note may be
taken of their quiet exertions, those who, after times
of strife and debate, have sought to erect and maintain educational institutions for the perpetuation of
liberty and truth, have done a work as needful and
as important as that of the valiant hero who, in the
hour of battle, stood forth as the champion of the
Lord.

Now, it is an evidence of the real greatness of
Elijah that he rendered both these kinds of service
to his country. For the reason which I have already
assigned, there is less said of the educational than of
the controversial portion of his work by the historian.
Yet, from sundry incidental allusions, we are led to
the conclusion that much of the Tishbite's labours,
especially in the later years of his life, were given to
the superintendence of the education of the sons of
the prophets throughout the land. The first mention
in Scripture of "schools of the prophets" is in the
history of Samuel, and it is probable that he was
himself the founder of that at Naioth. It is likely,
too, that David bestowed considerable attention on
these important seminaries, but, during the years that
intervened between Solomon and Ahab, we have no
reference made to them in the sacred books. And

it is not unreasonable to conclude that in the wide-
spread defection of the tribes, both in Judah and
Israel, from the Lord, they had fallen into neglect.
But, after the stirring controversy of his earlier
ministry, Elijah seems to have set himself to the
fostering, if not indeed to the refounding, of these
establishments. Either he himself set up such
schools at Gilgal, at Bethel, and at Jericho, or, finding
them existing there in a languishing condition, he
laboured to give them prosperity and permanence.
These ancient colleges were under the superintendence of a recognised prophet, who was called the
father, while the students were styled his children,
or sons. They were places of retirement adapted
for study and devotion ; yet they were not monas-
teries, as we now understand the word, for the
students were permitted to marry. They seem to
me to have resembled rather the seminary of the
ancient Culdee Church, the ruins of which still
awaken the interest of the traveller in the island of
Iona, and which was not a place of education merely,
but also a great missionary centre from which labourers
went forth in every direction to do the work of the
Lord. The subject of study at these institutions
was the law of Moses ; and along with that, but
subsidiary to it, attention was given to music and
sacred poetry, while, alike for purposes of recreation
and preparation for after-usefulness, the young men
were trained in various handicrafts, like those who
to-day are in the seminary of the venerable Spittler
near Basel, on the edge of the Black Forest.

In going to and fro among these schools, Elijah
found the labour and the happiness of his later

years. His form was familiar to the students, and they cherished for him a peculiar affection, which was as warmly reciprocated. So, when the close of his sojourn on the earth drew near, and it was intimated to him that he should be taken up to heaven by a whirlwind, it was natural that he should wish to pay a farewell visit to those interesting institutions in which were gathered the young men who were the nation's hope. Indeed, from the narrative before us, it would seem that he was already at Gilgal when he said to Elisha, who had been for years his constant attendant, " Tarry here, I pray thee, for the Lord hath sent me to Bethel." But a similar intimation to that which had been given to Elijah had been vouchsafed to the son of Shaphat, and he, resolved to abide by his master to the last, replied, " As the Lord liveth and as thy soul liveth, I will not leave thee." So they went both down to Bethel. As they approached the site of the sacred seminary, the well-known form of the man of God was recognised by the students, to whom also a knowledge of what was about to happen had been divinely communicated, and they came forth in a body to meet him with a greeting which was all the more tender because they knew it was their last. In response, we may imagine that he gave to them a few earnest counsels, bearing on their character and work ; but he said no word of that which was most heavy on their hearts; and eager to talk to some one on the subject, they whispered to Elisha, " Knowest thou that the Lord will take away thy master from thy head to-day ? " But he was as reserved as his master, and merely indicated that he was aware of what was about to take place, while he enjoined them to be silent, out of respect to the feelings of Elijah.

When they were about to depart from Bethel, the prophet renewed his request that Elisha should remain behind. It is difficult to account for this earnest wish of the Tishbite to be alone in the last and most glorious incident of his career. Perhaps its very solemnity made him desire to go apart from his fellows and his friends. We know that extreme agony or severe anxiety produces in the soul this longing for solitude, and it may be that at the other end of the scale the same law holds good, and that the highest raptures of triumph isolate a man from others as really as do the deepest trials. Or the prophet may have been prompted by a laudable modesty, and may have shrunk from seeming to make that a spectacle to others which was so full of honour to himself. Or, as in the case of Jesus, with the earnest suppliant, he may merely have designed to test and stimulate the faith of Elisha, so that at the critical moment he might be ready to receive the valuable legacy which he wished to leave him. But, whatever may have been his motive for asking Elisha to stay, his request was earnestly deprecated; and so they went on together to Jericho, where the incidents which had occurred at Bethel were substantially repeated. Again the students spoke privately to Elisha of his master's departure, and received an answer identical with that which he had given to their brethren. Again Elijah desired him to remain behind, and the former reply was given with deeper and more earnest emphasis.

So out from Jericho they two went on. Fifty students followed them till they came to an eminence which overlooked the Jordan, and there they remained " to view afar off." But the two pilgrims wended their way on toward the river, and when they reached the bank, Elijah, taking his mantle from his shoulders, and wrapping it up into a roll, smote the waters with it, and immediately they were parted hither and thither, so that they went over on dry ground. Up from the opposite bank they still held on their way ; and now, breaking the sacred silence which they had both maintained concerning that which was yet so vividly before their minds, Elijah said, "Ask what I shall do for thee, before I be taken away from thee;" to which Elisha made reply, "I pray thee, let a double portion of thy spirit be upon me."

How wisely, how divinely taught the son of Shaphat was ! He seeks not riches, nor worldly honour, nor power, nor anything that is in its nature earthly. He desires a double portion of his master's spirit. A double portion—the expression is peculiar. It does not mean that Elisha wished to be twice as great a prophet as his master had been. It is the formula which is used in the law to denote the portion of the first-born son in the family ; and its employment here by Elisha is very much as if he had spoken after this fashion : " Thou hast been visiting, at Gilgal, at Bethel, and at Jericho, thy spiritual sons; let me be as the first-born among them. Let me be, indeed, thy successor, the inheritor of thy spirit, and the continuer of thy work."

To this request Elijah made reply : "Thou has

asked a hard thing: nevertheless, if thou see me
taken from thee, it shall be so unto thee ; but if not,
it shall not be so." And still they went on and
talked : how we wish we had known the character of
their discourse, as thus they walked so consciously on
the confines of the unseen! Perhaps it was on high
and heavenly themes ; or, just as likely, it was on
some simple topic of daily life : we know not. Nor
is it an uninstructive feature in the narrative that we
are not informed concerning it ; for nothing—no, not
even his parting words—must interfere with the impression produced upon us by the manner of the prophet's
going hence. So, while they spake one with another,
a whirlwind came rushing up, a sudden change passed
over the heavens, and, lo ! in the bosom of the cloud
there was, as it were, a chariot of fire and horses of
fire :

> " The drivers were angels on horses of whiteness,
> And its burning wheels turned upon axles of brightness ;
> A seraph unfolded its doors bright and shining,
> All dazzling like gold of the seventh refining :
> On the arch of the rainbow the chariot is gliding,
> Through the paths of the thunder the horses are riding." [1]

And so, "caught up to meet the Lord in the air,"
Elijah went up into heaven, while Elisha was left
exclaiming, "My father, my father, the chariot of
Israel, and the horsemen thereof!" Then, gathering
up the mantle which had fallen from his ascending
master, he slowly retraced his steps ; and when he
came to the river, he smote the waters with the
official garment, crying, "Where is the Lord God of

---

[1] Hyslop's "Cameronian's Dream."

Elijah?" As he called, the river was again divided, and he went over. This was a sign to the students, who where still standing on the hill of Jericho, that he had succeeded to Elijah's dignity, and they went forth to meet him, and bowed themselves before him.

So much occurred on the earthly side of that storm-cloud which parted the Tishbite from his faithful follower ; but who can adequately imagine, much less describe, all that transpired on the heavenly ? In a moment, in the twinkling of an eye, the body of the prophet underwent that change which shall come upon the living at the day of Christ's appearing, for "flesh and blood cannot inherit the kingdom of God, neither doth corruption inherit incorruption." Then, with every demonstration of welcome, he is ushered into the presence of Him whom he had served so lovingly upon the earth. And as he is led on to his place of honour by the side of Enoch and of Moses, there swells from the attendant throng the glorious chorus, "Well done, good and faithful servant ! enter into the joy of thy Lord." Thou man of God, enjoy thy longed-for and well-earned repose ! Well for thee that thy Lord took thee not at thy word, when thou didst cry for death beneath the juniper-tree of the wilderness ! Bravely hast thou fought the battle of thy earthly life, and gloriously hast thou been taken, not through death, but over death, to wear "the crown of pure and everlasting and passionless renown !"

The history over which to-night we have come, unparalleled as it is in some respects, has yet in it material for practical applications that bear upon our modern life. We may learn from it, in the first place, the importance of the schools of the prophets in our land. Elijah paid no farewell visits to the great and noble of Israel ; but he could not leave the world without one more interview with the youths who were prosecuting their education at Gilgal, Bethel, and Jericho ; and that not simply because they were dear to him personally, as Timothy was to Paul, but because he recognised the momentous results to the nation at large of the work which lay before them in the coming years. They had in their hands much of the making of the character of the people for the next generation. And so, after having lovingly superintended their seminaries during the riper portion of his life, he went to say to them some memorable and impressive words, which would ever connect themselves in their minds with his translation to heaven. Now, from all this, we should be stirred up to take a deep, affectionate, and personal interest in the colleges and theological seminaries of our country. Those who to-day are the inmates of these institutions are to mould the thoughts and actions of the coming age. In the Harvards and Yales and Princetons of the present, you will find, sitting side by side, in the soft and plastic period of their youth, those who are to be the legislators and philosophers and ministers of religion in our land a few years hence, and who, when the present generation has passed away, will be the leaders of the community, giving it its intellectual, moral, and spiritual tone. There are, therefore, few institutions which have stronger claims upon our patriotism than the colleges of the land. Let them be liberally supported and generously endowed by the wealth of our merchants; and let the foremost men among us in every department count it the greatest honour that can be given them when they are asked to labour in such promising and important fields. Some time ago, it was my privilege to visit Oberlin, Ohio, and to preach to the assembled students of the college at that place. There were gathered together some twelve or fourteen hundred young people, and I have seldom been so deeply moved as when I rose to address them. I felt that there were very few places whence one's words would radiate farther, or sound longer, than from that pulpit; and I prayed that God might enable me to say something that would minister to His glory and the good of souls.

But if such be the importance of the words of a casual visitor, how much greater must be that of the teachings of their constant instructors. Surely, the best men in the land should be secured for the position of professors; and when secured, as I believe they very largely are, they ought to be liberally supported. Yet in this last respect the colleges of our country are greatly below the requirements of the age, and the salaries given to the professors, even in our oldest and most eminent institutions, are miserably inadequate. Let our men of wealth in the great cities look to this immediately; for the vigour of our educational institutions has a very intimate connection with the stability of our political constitution and the prosperity of our commercial enterprises. It gladdened the heart of Agassiz when one of our own citizens gave a whole island for the prosecution of his scientific pursuits; and though he did not live long to enjoy the gift, we feel thankful now that it was not delayed until it would have been too late.[1] Let others imitate this noble example ; for education elevates and refines the nation, and our colleges are the true centres of influence in the land.

But if it be important for our citizens to look after our colleges, it is even more so for our churches to give heed to the theological seminaries of the land. It is true, indeed, that the Christian people help very largely to make the minister who comes among them by the tone and temper of their daily lives ; but it is also a fact, that the minister does much to make the Church by his teaching and example. Now, our theological seminaries are making the ministers of the future. From them are to come forth the men who shall by and by occupy our pulpits, who shall lay the foundations of our churches, in the new districts of the West, and who shall take up and carry forward the labours of our foreign missionaries. The mantles of our present pastors and preachers are ere long to fall on the shoulders of those who are to-day the students of our seminaries. Surely, therefore, it well becomes us to give the most fostering care to these interesting and noble institutions. Let us get for them the ablest men on whom we can lay our hands ; let us give liberally, so that the occupant of a chair shall not feel that he is a whit behind the very chiefest of our city pastors in emolument ; and let us statedly and steadily remember them in our prayers, that God may pour upon them His richest benediction. There are few nobler positions on the earth than that

[1] I have recently heard that the Penikese experiment has failed, for the time. Will no one step into the breach, and carry the enterprise into permanent prosperity ?

occupied by him who trains the ministers of the Church of Christ; and so when we have seen lately one of the most honoured and successful of the ministers [1] of this city, after a pastorate of forty years, consecrating the maturity of his experience, the wealth of his resources, the culture of his intellect, and the reputation of his life, to the work of the professorial chair, we have felt that it was all that was needed to give the ornamental capital to the polished pillar of his public life. May God preserve him long in his new and noble sphere, and may the influence of this act of his give to our theological seminaries throughout the land a firmer hold on the minds and hearts of the members of the Christian Church !

But, in the second place, we may learn from this history that there is commonly a correspondence between the general character of a life and the nature of its close. Elijah did not see death; but though we might not have anticipated for him such a termination of his earthly career as that which we have to-night attempted to describe, we yet can see a special fitness in it as the close of such a life as his. His history was one of storm. He came in before Ahab, at first, as with the rush of the hurricane; and in the divine symbolism of the Horeb vision, we might describe his ministry as consisting successively in whirlwind and earthquake and fire. Fitly, therefore, did such a one go up in a whirlwind to heaven. Now, of course, in so far as his departure from the

---

[1] These words were written just after the acceptance by Dr. William Adams of the Presidency of Union Theological Seminary, and I delight in this opportunity of weaving my little "mountain daisy" into the chaplet that adorns his brow.

earth was a translation, it was exceptional, and, save in the case of Enoch, it has had no parallel; but in so far as this sort of close to his life was appropriate to the general character of the work he did on earth, it was only another instance of the fact that the nature of a man's death is determined by the kind of life which has preceded it. Your Great-heart, who has gone through the world vanquishing every foe in the might of the Lord Jesus, finds the Jordan dry when he goes over, and has not so much a death as a translation. Your Hopeful, who has been walking all along his pilgrimage in the sunshine of God's countenance, is of good cheer also when he goes into the river. In the rich old language of John Bunyan, he "feels the bottom, and it is good." While your timid Christian, who has all along been troubled with quivering misgivings, and has had to go shuddering through many a valley of shadow, will be full of anxiety when he is in the article of death, and will be thankful for any word of promise which a brother may whisper in his ear. But you do not think any the less of him because of that; nor do you imagine that there is, on that account, any less hope in his death. You are sorry for his own sake, because you wish he had more peace and, indeed, some triumph; but you recollect what has been the character of his experience throughout, and you begin to see that the manner of his departure is taking the same hue. We must have the life of an Elijah, if we are to have a translation at its close; and it is noteworthy that, so far as we know anything of it from the fragment of Jude, Enoch's was just such a life of struggle and protest against abounding iniquity as that of the Tishbite. Paul could say with ease, " To die is gain," after he had been able to say, " To me to live is Christ." So if we wish to have an experience of peace and hope and triumph in the hour of our departure, we must get out of our despondency now, and begin to " live Christ " in the cheerfulness of his happiness as well as in the purity of his holiness. In any case, just as the river takes with it to the sea the colour which its waters have contracted from the soil over which it has flowed throughout its course, so our death experiences will partake of the character, be it sombre or cheerful, which our lives have had. There may be exceptional instances, when, after long-continued despondency, there comes light at evening-time ; but these are exceptional. The best means of having light at death is to walk in the light through life. Try this, my brethren, and you will find that He who met Elijah with his chariot of fire will not be far from you when you close your eyes on this sublunary scene.

We may note, in the third place, the connection which subsists between strong faith in the invisible life and the power of a public ministry. When Elisha requested a double portion of Elijah's spirit, his master made reply, " Thou hast asked a hard thing ; nevertheless, if thou see me when I am taken from thee, it shall be so unto thee ; but if not, it shall not be so." That is to say, the securing of that on which Elisha's heart was set depended on his seeing Elijah's ascension. Now, have you thought on the reason of that appended condition? Where the record is silent, we may conjecture ; but we must not dogmatise. It is with diffidence, therefore, that I venture to sug-

gest an explanation. Still the suggestion may itself
be profitable, whether or not you accept the theory
on which it is based. The sight of Elijah's ascension
gave to his servant a firmer and more vivid faith
in the reality of the unseen life than he ever had
before. Had Elijah simply died like another man,
no more lively sense of the invisible would have been
given to Elisha than that which he had received at
the death-bed of any other friend. But when he saw
the prophet taken from his side alive, he felt as he
had never felt before regarding the other state of
existence. Wherever he had gone, the prophet was
living, and if he had gone, as he was sure he had, to
Jehovah, then a new emphasis was given to the words
which used to be so often on his lips, "Jehovah
liveth," and in that faith in Jehovah as the living one
lay the power of the spirit of Elijah. He did not
think of the prophet as one thinks, in spite of himself
sometimes, of a near relative who is dead. He
thought of him as alive, and that gave new reality in
his soul to his belief in the living Jehovah. Hence
it was with no misgivings, and not at all as an experiment to see how he would succeed, but in the
strongest faith, that he cried out, "Where is the Lord
God of Elijah?" And the power which he then
received continued with him throughout his entire
career.

We have a similar thing in the history of the
Christian apostles. Their sight of the Lord's ascension gave life and power to their labours in His
cause. No doubt the Spirit came down upon them
on Pentecost, but their prayer for the Spirit derived
life and earnestness from their knowledge of the fact

that Jesus had gone alive into heaven ; and you cannot read, in even the most cursory manner, the first
chapters of the Acts of the Apostles without feeling
how vivid was their sense of the fact that Christ was
living. This it was that gave life to their prayers,
earnestness to their discourses, and energy to their
characters. Their devotions were no mere pious
meditations, but they were like letters sent by one
to another whom he knows to be interested in his
doing ; and all their references to Him in public
were to one who was very real and very near to them.
Thus on them also the Spirit of power came down
through their faith in the unseen, quickened and
focalised as that was by their sight of their Lord in
the act and article of His ascension. Now, if we
would have more power, we must aim first at securing this faith in the invisible. It was said of one
that as he prayed he spoke as if God was so near,
and talked with him so really and confidingly, that
those who were beside him found themselves almost
looking round to see where God was. It was said
of another that he preached as if the Lord Jesus were
standing just by his side. Brethren, when we have
this faith in the real, living nearness to us of the
unseen Jehovah, we, too, shall have the Spirit of
power, and find upon our shoulders—shall I make
bold to say it?—the mantle, not of a prophet or
apostle, but of the ascended Christ Himself.

Let us learn, in the fourth place, the value of a
good man to his country. Elisha called his master
"the chariot of Israel and the horsemen thereof,"
implying that he was the true national defence,
better to Israel than all the pomp and circumstance

of a military host. And that this was no exaggerated
estimate, we may learn from the valuable services
which Elisha himself rendered to the ten tribes when
they were sorely menaced by the Syrian hosts. But
though his gift of prophecy and miracle made Elijah
peculiarly serviceable to Israel, it is as true to-day as
it was in his time that the real strength and rampart
of a nation are the good men that belong to it.
Character is power; and, therefore, that is the
strongest nation that has most of purity and morality
and nobleness in the lives of its people. "Providence," said Bonaparte on one occasion, somewhat
sneeringly, "is generally on the side of the strongest
battalions." Be it so ; but has not the moral character of the soldiery much to do with the strength
of the battalion which they form ? And even, apart
from military prowess altogether, are not the prayers
of the people of God more powerful than all the en-
ginery of war. "There was a little city, and few men
within it ; and there came a great king against it, and
besieged it, and built great bulwarks against it. Now
there was found in it a poor wise man, and he by his
wisdom delivered the city ; yet no man remembered
that same poor man. Then said I, Wisdom is better
than strength : nevertheless the poor man's wisdom is
despised, and his words are not heard."[1] Thus spake
Solomon thousands of years ago, and the world has
not yet learned the lesson of his words. Wisdom is
better than strength. Character is the noblest
strength. Oh that the men of this land to-day would
but give good heed to this neglected truth ! It is not

---

[1] Ecclesiastes ix. 14-16.

armies or navies, or diplomacy or wealth, that is to
defend us from attack without, or from perfidy
within.   It is character that is a nation's real grandeur
and true palladium.   But what makes the noblest
character?   Is it not belief in and obedience to the
Lord Jesus Christ?   Thus piety is the loftiest
patriotism, and the army of Christian men and
women are more to our land than all earthly soldiery
or military defence.

Finally, let us learn that though men are removed
from earth, God remains to strengthen and bless His
people.   Elijah ascends, but God, through Elisha, is
as gracious as before.   So when statesmen and
ministers of religion are taken away, the Lord is still
left to the State and to the Church.   They did not
take Jehovah with them when they left the earth, and
we can still sing, " God lives ; blessed be our Rock,
and let the God of our salvation be exalted."   Nor
is the application of this truth restricted to national
or ecclesiastical life.   It is true in our homes as well
as in our churches.   The head of the household may
be removed ; but the God of Elijah remains, who
fed His servant by the ravens, and made provision for
the widow and the orphan in the home of Zarephath.
Therefore He will provide for and comfort the
bereaved who put their trust in Him.   Haply there
may be some one here to-night mourning over some
such loss, and crying, not in the assurance of firm
faith, but in the sadness of despondency, " Where is
the Lord God of Elijah?"   Let such a one take
courage from the bearing of Elisha here, and go
forward.   True, the river of some great difficulty may
lie before thee, and thou mayest fear to advance ;

but Jehovah will open up thy way. He who tenderly fed His desponding servant when he lay beneath the juniper-tree will not forsake thee. He is near to all that call upon Him—that call upon Him in truth. Therefore, call upon Him in the day of trouble : "He will deliver thee, and thou shalt glorify His name."

XIII.

ELIJAH ON THE MOUNT.

LUKE ix. 30, 31.

AN Alpine traveller has told us how, one day, he set out from Geneva, in a dense and dripping fog, to climb one of the hills in the range of the Grand Salève ; and how, after ascending for some hours, he came out above the mist, and saw the cloudless sky above him, and around him on every hand the snowy battlement of the glorious mountains. In the valley lay the fog, like a waveless ocean of white vapour ; and as he stood on the overhanging crags, he could hear the chime of bells, the lowing of cattle, and the sounds of labour coming up from the villages that lay invisible beneath ; while now and then, darting up out of the cloudy sea, there came a bird, which, after delighting itself a while in the joyous sunshine, and singing a glad song to greet the unexpected brightness, dived down again and disappeared. Now what that brief time of unclouded radiance was to the bird which had left the drizzling dulness of the lower world beneath it, that was the experience of the transfiguration to our Lord Jesus. His earthly life, as a whole, was spent in the valley, beneath the clouds of suffering and sorrow ; and it was only at rare intervals that He emerged above it, and stood on the mountain-top in the glorious majesty of His native Godhead. Of such occasions, that of the transfiguration was, by far, the grandest. There was, indeed, nothing precisely like it in His whole earthly career. It stands alone, even among the marvels of His history, rising above them with as much magnificence as does the mountain on which it took place above the surrounding plain.

And yet, because it was singular, we are not to conclude that it was the most marvellous incident of His life; for when we remember that He was divine, nothing will seem more natural than that His glory should be thus transcendent. Viewed from the heavenly and divine side of His nature, His transfiguration was indeed the least surprising thing in His experience. There is nothing astonishing in the idea that God should be surrounded with light as with a garment: but that He should have taken human nature; that He should have lain in the cradle of infancy, and wrought at the carpenter's bench, and been crucified on a malefactor's cross—these are the marvels. Accordingly, the glorified saints who were with Him on the Mount expressed no surprise at seeing Him "pavilioned with splendour;" but they conversed with Him on the decease which He should accomplish at Jerusalem as on the thing which was at once most amazing to them and most interesting to Him.

But we must not anticipate, or begin to expound the meaning of the transfiguration, until we have endeavoured to set it in its true perspective by placing before you its antecedents and surroundings.

Some six or eight days before, Peter had made his
noble confession of faith : "Thou art the Christ, the
Son of the living God ;" and almost immediately
thereafter the Lord made formal announcement to His
followers of His approaching death and resurrection.
This took them all by surprise ; for though, with His
accustomed impulsiveness, Peter was the first to
speak, he was yet only giving utterance to the sentiments of them all when he said, " That be far from
Thee, Lord ; this shall not be unto Thee." But, to
their still greater amazement, this response of the son
of Jonas, which seemed to them so full of kindness,
was met with perhaps the severest reproof that ever
came from the Master's lips : "Get thee behind
me, Satan ; thou art an offence unto me : for thou
savourest not the things that be of God, but those
that be of men."

This conversation, peculiar as it was, both in its
theme and in its manner, must have been still fresh
in the memory of the disciples, when about a week
after, at the close of a day spent in the service of
humanity, the Lord sought rest of spirit in fellowship
with His Father. For this purpose He betook Himself to a mountain, and, leaving nine of His disciples
in the valley, He took with Him those three who
were always chosen by Him for special privilege or
arduous duty. When they reached the summit, it
would seem that night had darkened down upon
them, and Jesus gave Himself to prayer, while His
companions, worn out by the fatigues of the ascent,
were "heavy with sleep." But having had former
experience that, when they were thus selected from
the others, something unusual was sure to happen,

they bravely battled with their drowsiness and kept awake (for the word rendered "when they were awake" properly means "having kept awake"). Nor was their watchfulness unrewarded, for, as Jesus, "filled the silent night" with His supplications, a wondrous transformation passed upon Him. "His face did shine as the sun," and "His raiment became shining, exceeding white as snow; so as no fuller on earth can white them."

This light was not reflected upon Him from without, but it was radiated from the divinity that dwelt within Him; it was the breaking through of the glory, which commonly was veiled by the flesh of His humanity. But as they looked on, and their dazzled eyes became accustomed to the shining splendour, they saw that their Master was not alone. "There appeared with Him two men," wearing the garb of glorified humanity, whom, by some peculiar indications, they identified as Moses and Elijah, and they talked with Him on the subject of His death upon the cross. What a theme for such high converse! How we long to have but one golden sentence from that glorious triumvirate on such a subject! Little wonder that Peter, as he listened, desired that the precious privilege should be indefinitely prolonged, and said, as he saw the celestial deputation about to depart: "Lord, it is good for us to be here: if Thou wilt, let us make here three tabernacles; one for Thee, and one for Moses, and one for Elias." But, after all, his request was one of ignorance. There was a world to be redeemed and converted; there were sufferers in the valley waiting to be relieved; there was work to be done, which

needed the self-sacrifice and exertion alike of his
Lord, of himself, and of his apostolic companions;
and so, even as he spake, there came the mystic
shekinah cloud, the emblem of Jehovah's presence,
wherein He was in part revealed, and in part also
concealed, and overshadowed them. As it settled
down upon them, they were filled with holy reverence,
and there came to them a voice from the excellent
glory, " This is My beloved Son, in whom I am well
pleased ; hear ye Him." Then, as it passed away,
and the clear shining of the silent stars was seen by
them once more, Jesus was found alone ; and when
the day broke they descended to the valley, with a
new and deeper adoration of Him who had called
them to be His followers.

Now, if I were to attempt to expound the full
significance of this remarkable event in the Gospel
history, there are many methods which I might adopt.
I might look at it in its relation to the Saviour, to
the glorified beings who stood by His side, to the
apostles, and to the Church at large ; or I might take
it as furnishing one of the most striking proofs of the
deity of Him who came into the world to save
sinners ; or I might regard it as establishing the
reality of the unseen state of existence, and the fact
that the inhabitants of heaven are deeply interested
in the progress of the cause of Christ upon the earth.
But, coming upon it as I do now, in connection with
our study of the life and times of Elijah the Tishbite,
I am compelled to narrow the range of my observations, and look at it from that point of view which
will best enable us to understand the presence of
Elijah with Moses on the occasion. This, however,

will be no disadvantage in the end, inasmuch as, by so doing, we shall grasp the central significance of the scene, which, while it was truly historic, was also designed to be parabolic and instructive.

Now, if we attentively consider it, we shall discover that the central truth of the transfiguration was this : Christ glorified in connection with His death. The disciples, in their ignorance and prejudice, had supposed that it would be a dishonour to their Lord to be put to death ; and they looked upon such an event as a virtual extinguishing of the hopes which they had permitted themselves to cherish. They fancied that their Master had come to establish an earthly kingdom, wherein they should hold places of peculiar honour ; and so, when they heard Him speak of His decease, they accounted that He was preparing for defeat, and that they were about to be covered with confusion. Hence they preferred to hear no more about it ; the subject was one which was full of pain and grief to them. So far from wreathing Him with glory, the death of their Master, in their estimation, would darken Him with dishonour, in which, as His chosen companions, they would have to share. But here, as He speaks with Moses and Elijah on this very topic, His countenance is radiant with brightness, and they show an intensity of interest in its accomplishment which furnishes a remarkable contrast to the hasty deprecation in which Peter had indulged. Thus there was given to the disciples a new view of that decease, from the very thought of which they had so revolted at the first, and they were taught to connect it, not with shame, but with honour.

Let us learn the lesson with them. We cannot

comprehend the transfiguration if we dissever it from
Calvary; for the glory that radiated from Jesus on
the Mount was but the first faint foretaste of that
celestial honour which would be conferred on Him
when He should ascend from His completed work, and
take His seat on the right hand of the Majesty on
high.

Tell us, ye who would have us believe that the
death of Jesus was a mere martyrdom, like that of
Stephen, why here Christ is so glorified as He speaks
concerning it, and why these great ones, so long the
denizens of heaven, should appear on earth to talk
with Him of its accomplishment. Why did they not
rather discourse of the morality He taught, of the
holiness He manifested, or of the originality of the
doctrines which He promulgated? Rest assured, my
brethren, that, wherever the cross of Christ may be
undervalued and the sacrifice of Christ ignored, it is
not in heaven; and the very same motive that urges
the redeemed before the throne to sing "Worthy is
the Lamb that was slain," impelled these two representatives of the Church triumphant here to speak
with Jesus of the "decease which He should accomplish at Jerusalem.

That death upon the cross was not a mere personal
matter, concerning only Jesus Christ Himself. It
involved in it the dearest interests of saints already
in heaven, and of sinners down to the last hour of
time. It was, indeed, the most important event in
the history of the universe; the great central fact in
the annals of humanity; the meeting-place of the two
eternities. By it Jesus consummated His sacrificial
work; satisfied the law and justice of God in the room

of sinners, triumphed over all His adversaries, and laid the foundation of that kingdom which is to be universal in its extent and eternal in its duration. All this, of course, would not appear, at first, in connection with it. When men saw Him hanging on the cross, and heard Him cry, in heaviness of spirit, " My God, my God, why hast Thou forsaken me ? " it might seem to them, it did seem to them, that He was vanquished ; but when He rose from the tomb on the morning of the third day, He was declared a conqueror, and was seen to be the deliverer of His people from sin and death.

This, I doubt not, was the view which Moses and Elijah got of it as thus they stood in glory, and spake of it with the transfigured Christ ; for there is a peculiarity in the original expression that is, to my mind, singularly suggestive. Literally rendered, Luke's words are, " They spake of the exodus which He should accomplish at Jerusalem." It may be a mere fancy, indeed ; yet as that is the term which, in the Greek version of the Old Testament, even as in our own English Bible, is the name of the Second Book of Moses, that tells of the leading-forth of the tribes of Israel from their house of bondage, I cannot help thinking that these two ancient worthies had come to regard the death of Christ as a grander exodus than that of which Moses was the leader ; and whether they had or not, there is no doubt whatever that such was really the fact. That of Moses delivered from the bondage of the Egyptian taskmasters, whose lash galled only the body ; this of Jesus rescues from the slavery of sin, whose chains of habit are coiled around the soul. That of Moses was achieved by the de-

struction of Pharaoh and his host; this of Jesus by
the overthrow of Satan and his legions. That of
Moses was accomplished by the mere attribute of
power, through the instrumentality of his wonder-
working rod; this of Jesus was wrought out by love,
which sacrificed itself for the good of sinners on the
cross of Calvary. That of Moses emancipated but
one nation; this has introduced a great multitude,
whom no man can number, out of all peoples, and
kindreds, and ages, into " the glorious liberty of the
children of God." Hence, if it be true, as Bunsen
says, that " history itself was born on the night when
Moses led forth his countrymen from the land of
Goshen," it is no less true that a new era in the annals of humanity was introduced at Calvary when
our Great Deliverer cried, not in weakness, but in
triumph, " It is finished ! "

The bush burned, but it was not consumed; yea,
in the midst of the flame, its green leaves kept their
verdure, intensifying the wonder of the spectacle,
whereon Mosed gazed with rapt reverence and in un-
sandaled feet. But here is a wonder greater still;
for while the fire played round the man Christ Jesus,
the divinity within Him still kept its indestructible
features, and gave to the spectacle at once its mystery and its majesty.

Brethren, there are two transfigurations : that of the
Mount, and that of the cross; and it is impossible to
understand either, save in the light of the other. He
who was on the Mount was still the Man of Sorrows,
and He who was on the cross was still the Divine Son.
The death on the cross gave its glory to the mountain
scene; the declaration on the Mount makes the death

all-radiant with triumph, in spite of the blackened heavens and the hooting multitude. To the heavenly hosts the scene upon the Mount was natural, and that on the cross was the transfiguration; to us the death was human, and the mountain scene divine; but, in reality, the two are one, or, rather, they are but opposite sides of the one great mystery of godliness, God manifest in the flesh; and both alike are transcendently glorious.

But I must pass on to remark, in the second place, how Christ, glorified through His death, reflects back a radiance on Moses and Elijah. At first sight we are disposed to wonder that, out of all the glorified ones in heaven, these two should have been chosen to be present on this great occasion; and, doubtless, had the selection been made on merely personal grounds, it might have fallen upon others, such as Abraham, the father of the faithful, or Daniel, the man greatly beloved. But the delegation was sent for public rather than personal reasons; and in the official position which these two had held on earth we find the explanation of their appearance here. Moses is inseparably associated with the law which was given to Israel through his instrumentality; while Elijah (as we have seen) was distinguished for his zeal in reforming his countrymen, and bringing them back to the observance of the precepts which Moses had commanded, but which Ahab and the people had disregarded.

It has been supposed by many indeed, that Elijah was here as the representative of the prophets; but though, in the broad sense of speaking in the name and by the inspiration of God, Elijah was certainly a prophet, yet there is a clear distinction between him and Isaiah, or Ezekiel, or Daniel, or Zechariah. These last all looked forward, and had much to say of the great coming Deliverer, and the kingdom which He was to establish on the earth. But the work of Elijah was not so much a preparation for the future as an earnest effort for the restoration of the past. It was with him through all his public life, as it was that day on Carmel, when he repaired the altar which had been broken down. During his whole public ministry he was seeking to build up a ruined altar, and to bring back again the nation to its observance of the Mosaic ritual.

Thus it was most fit that he should stand by the side of Moses, especially when now, as the result of Christ's death, the necessity for the perpetuation of the Mosaic economy was about to cease, and a new and better, because more spiritual, dispensation was to be introduced. They were here to do homage to the Lord Jesus as the new king ; they were here to set an example to the Jews of confidence in the Christ who had come to abrogate the law by " the bringing in of a better hope."

But observe that they were here *in glory.* Now, that of course was a literal fact. They came wearing the nature of the blessed immortals in the heavenly world. Of that there can be no doubt. Yet this glory had also a parabolic significance, and we see in it the illumination which is given to the whole system of Jewish worship by the death of Christ. Nothing can well be more unmeaning or enigmatical than a transparency when you put it upon a mantel-shelf, or hang it against a dark background. But take it up,

and look at it with the bright sunshine behind it, and
what a transfiguration ensues ! Forthwith some ex-
quisite work of art comes into view, and lines of
beauty and significance, which you would never otherwise have thought of, force themselves upon your attention.

Now is it not just so with the whole history and
economy of Moses? In themselves considered, the
Books of Exodus, Numbers, Leviticus, and Deuteronomy are not the most interesting in the Scriptures ;
but take them and read them in the light of Christ,
and what a new world of meaning is there then revealed ! Peruse the Book of Exodus in the light of
the Gospel history and of Christian experience, and
say if Moses is not made thereby a sharer in the glory
of the transfigured Christ? Egypt, Marah, the manna,
the wilderness, the water from the rock, the serpent
of brass, the parted Jordan, the long-desired Canaan,
with its milk and honey, all acquire a new significance,
and the book is henceforth an old edition of the
" Pilgrim's Progress," in black letter, and with quaint
engravings, such as strike us more than the finished
pictures of a modern artist.

So, again, with the ritual which Moses introduced.
Take Christ for a background to that transparency,
and you have the Epistle to the Hebrews, so marvellous
in its beauty and so matchless in its glory. The tabernacle, with its furniture ; the festivals, with their
peculiar surroundings ; the ark, with its cherubim continually gazing on the blood-stained mercy-seat, as the
angels desire to look into the sufferings of Christ and
the glory that should follow—all are irradiated with
new lustre, a lustre reflected from the face of Christ.

Take one example : In the ordinances prescribed for the great Day of Atonement, we find that two goats were to be designated by lot ; the one was to be slain, and the other, bearing sin on its devoted head, was to be led by the hand of a fit man into the wilderness.   It seems a singular and unmeaning thing ; but when you look at the whole in the light of Christ, these two goats, like the two pictures in the modern stereoscope, blend into one finely relieved and beautifully distinct image of " the Lamb of God taking away the sin of the world."   So it is with all the others.

And so do we find it also with Elijah.   You have wondered, as, indeed, I have myself, at the deeply suggestive lessons for modern life which we have received from this old history of the Tishbite ; but here is the explanation as we read it with the Son of Righteousness for a background.   Nothing can well be duller or more dingy than the appearance of a cathedral window to one who is looking on it from the outside of the building ; but when you enter and gaze at it from within, the whole is aglow with beauty.

Now, most people read the history of Elijah much as they would that of some old hermit, and they get little out of it.   We have tried to read it in the light of the Gospel, and, as we have done so, we have seen that Elijah is a sharer of the glory of the transfigured Christ.   We saw Calvary from Carmel ; in the still small voice which we heard at Horeb we discerned the merciful accents of Him whom the Magdalene recognised when, at the door of the sepulchre, He said unto her " Mary !"   And in the ascension of the faithful prophet we descried a far-off prediction of the day when to those on His right hand the Judge shall

say, " Come, ye blessed of my Father, inherit the kingdom prepared for you from the foundation of the
world." Thus the glory of Christ illuminates Moses
and Elias ; and as we read their pages, so irradiated,
we are to ourselves as if we stood with the privileged
three on the Mount of Transfiguration, and we, too,
are constrained to say, " It is good for us to be here."

But now, advancing another step, behold how, as
Moses and Elijah are thus glorified by Christ, they
retire from view, and give place to Him. When the
vision was past, the disciples saw no man, save
" Jesus only ;" nay, when the two were in the act of
departing, the cloud came down, and a voice from the
midst of it proclaimed, " This is my beloved Son, in
whom I am well pleased." Thus the servants fall
back before the Son whom the Father solemnly in-
troduces to the world, and commends to its attention,
saying, in effect, " Ye have heard Moses and Elijah,
and ye did well to hear them ; for they were my servants. But now a greater than either has come to
you, even mine only begotten and well-beloved Son ;
therefore hear Him."

Thus Moses and Elijah, when rightly understood,
lead up to Christ, and leave us with Him. Their
function was pedagogic, or educational, and it is over
when men come to Christ. The moment the Mosaic
ritual is seen in its true bearing on the Gospel, it
ceases to be binding on the conscience, and men are
enjoined to take the law at the Redeemer's lips.
Hence this vision, rightly understood, was designed
to make the transition from the law to the Gospel
easy for the disciples and their earliest converts among
the Jews.

But in this last " Hear Him " there are a breadth
and an intensity of injunction that concern us also.
Hear Him ! My brother, have you opened your ears
to any of His words? Have you listened to His faithful warnings, His tender expostulations, His gracious
invitations, His precious promises, His consoling utterances? Is it so that you have an ear for the classic
dramatist, or the political orator, or the scientific
lecturer, or the concord of sweet sounds that came
first from the heart and brain of some Beethoven or
Mozart, while yet you will not listen to the Son of
God? Go back to the days of His flesh, and be reproved by the words which fell from the lips of the
officers sent by His enemies to apprehend Him, as
they said, "Never man spake like this man." Go
back, and learn from the masses of His own day how
much you miss in turning away from Him; for "the
common people heard Him gladly." Even as artistic
productions, His discourses are unrivalled in the litera-
ture of earth. Where will you find such fertility and
beauty of illustration, wedded to such simplicity of
style and massiveness of thought? Who so original
as the prophet of Nazareth? Who so authoritative
with the authority of truth? Who so sympathetic as
He who bore our griefs and carried our sorrows?
But that is a low ground on which to ask your attention to His words. He is the Son of God, and His
utterances concern you. "Except ye repent, ye shall
all likewise perish." Impenitent sinner, hear that!
"Except a man be born again, he cannot see the
kingdom of God." Hypocrite, with the fair show and
the false heart, hear that! "God so loved the world,
that He gave His only begotten Son, that whosoever

believeth in Him should not perish, but have ever-lasting life." Despairing sinner, you who fear that God has cast you off, hear that "whosoever," and grasp it, and by it lift yourself up to the "whosoever believeth." "Him that cometh unto Me, I will in no-wise cast out." Doubting sinner, hesitating whether you will be received if you come, hear that! "Let not your heart be troubled, ye believe in God, believe also in me." Desponding Christian, who art carrying the burden of some sore sorrow, hear that! "I am the Resurrection and the Life : he that believeth in Me, though he were dead, yet shall he live ; and he that liveth, and believeth in Me, shall never die." Bereaved Christians, hear that! Take the Sermon on the Mount, all ye who are seeking for a directory for life, and as you read it forget not these closing words : "Whosoever heareth these sayings of mine, and doeth them, I will liken him unto a wise man, which built his house upon a rock : and the rain descended, and the floods came, and the winds blew, and beat upon that house ; and it fell not : for it was founded upon a rock. And every one that heareth these sayings of mine, and doeth them not, shall be likened unto a foolish man, which built his house upon the sand : and the rain descended, and the floods came, and the winds blew, and beat upon that house, and it fell : and great was the fall of it."

I have, to-night, but one thought for my closing lesson. See here the reality of the future life. Elijah was with Christ more than eight hundred years after his translation, and Moses more than twelve hundred after his burial in "Nebo's lonely mountain." As Elijah did not die, we know that he

appeared in glorified humanity ; and as it is said that
two men talked with Jesus, we infer that the body of
Moses had been raised in anticipation of the general
resurrection.   If this view be accepted, then it may
help to explain an obscure passage in the Epistle of
Jude, where we read that " Michael the archangel
contended with the devil, disputing about the body of
Moses."   But however that may have been, here are
two men living hundreds of years after the death of
the one and the translation of the other.

Here, therefore, we have one of the most striking
proofs of the reality of the world unseen.   We must
either give up our faith in the historic verity of this
narrative, or we must accept it as an incontrovertible
evidence of the fact that there is a life beyond this.
Now, I will not argue here.   I know you believe that
there is such a state.   But what provision are you
making for it.   Where will you be in it?   Here,
centuries after the finishing of their earthly course,
we find Moses and Elijah in such circumstances as
warrant us to believe that they were happy in the
presence of their God.   In a short time each of us
shall be as they, with the mystery of death behind
us ; but shall we be as they also, joyful in the
heavenly inheritance ?   The first moment after death
—that will settle it all.   What will that be ?   Nay, I
am wrong.   We are settling even now what that first
moment shall be.   How are you settling it, my
hearer ?   If you are living in sin, you are settling
that, when you leave the body, the first and continued
experience of your soul shall be that of perdition : if
you are living in Christ, you are settling that, when
your spirit leaves its fleshly tabernacle, you shall have

"a building of God; a house not made with hands, eternal in the heavens." Which is it?

Now the God of Peace, that brought again from the dead our Lord Jesus, that great Shepherd of the sheep, through the blood of the everlasting covenant, make you perfect in every good work to do His will, working in you that which is well pleasing in His sight, through Jesus Christ, to whom be glory for ever and ever. Amen.

INDEX.

———o———

RAVENS feeding Elijah, 27 ; reasons for holding by the received opinion regarding, 28, 29.

Reformers vindicated from modern objections, 18 ; often characterised by tenderness as well as strength, 58.

Rejection of God punished, both under the Gospel and the law, 195–199.

Resurrection of Christ, relation of, to the raising of the widow's son, 63–65.

Retribution certainty of, under God's government, 181–183.

Robertson's, Rev. F. W., sermons, referred to, 132, 139.

SACRIFICE of Elijah, relation of, to that of Christ, 106, 107.

Sailors, piety among, 86.

Saunder's, Frederick, "Evenings with the Sacred Poets," referred to, 37.

Selfishness of the ungodly, 89.

Self-prominence, evil of, 141.

Selling one's self to work iniquity, 179, 180.

Servant of God must deal with men according to their characters, 94, 95.

Shirley, Rev. W. W., quoted from, 4.

Sidney, Sir Philip, an illustration of benevolence, 50.

Sin, growth of, insidious, 15, 16 ; price of, 179.

Sinners cannot run away from God, 192.

Slaughter of the priests of Baal vindicated, 112.

Smith's "Dictionary of the Bible," quoted from, 11, 30.

Soldiers, piety of, 82.

Solitude, value of, 25, 26.

Special training needed for special work, 159.

Spirit, double portion of Elijah's, meaning of, 208.

Stanley, Dean, quoted from, 42, 59.

Stevenson, Rev. W. F., quoted from, 37.

Sunday Magazine, incident from, 49.

TAYLOR, Isaac, referred to, 125.

Tell-el-Kusis, hill of the priests, 99.

Temporal things provided by God as well as spiritual, 32.

Tenderness of God, 142, 183, 199.

Tennyson, Alfred, quoted from, 26, 60.

Theological seminaries, importance of, 213, 214.

PRINTED BY BALLANTYNE, HANSON AND CO.
EDINBURGH AND LONDON